With lov.

Beth

xxx

A MARY FORD PUBLICATION

CHILDREN'S CAKES

CHILDREN'S CAKES

MARY FORD TUBE NO's SHOWING THEIR SHAPES

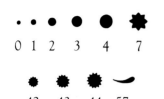

0 1 2 3 4 7

42 43 44 57

The above are icing tube shapes used in this book. Please note that these are Mary Ford tubes, but comparable tubes may be used. All the tools and equipment required to complete the cakes and decorations in this book are obtainable from the Mary Ford Cake Artistry Centre, 28-30 Southbourne Grove, Bournemouth, Dorset BH6 3RA, England or local stockists.

Printed and bound in Hong Kong

ISBN 0 946429 35 9

Mary Ford stresses the importance of all aspects of cake artistry, but gives special emphasis to the basic ingredients and unreservedly recommends the use of Tate and Lyle Icing Sugar.

CONTENTS

THE AUTHOR

Mary Ford has been teaching her craft for over two decades, through personal contact and her books, and during that time she has gained a world-wide reputation for expertise and imagination combined with common sense and practical teaching skills. Her first book "101 Cake Designs" is an international best-seller and an acknowledged bible for the cake decorator. Her subsequent books have all used the step-by-step approach with the emphasis on numerous colour illustrations and brief editorial advice. This book, as with all the other Mary Ford titles, is the result of close collaboration between Mary (designing and making the cakes) and her husband, Michael (photographing and production). Their joint efforts bring an added clarity to the tried and tested Mary Ford teaching method.

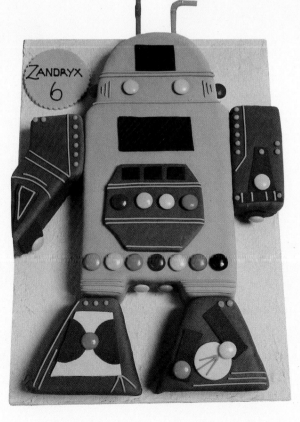

INTRODUCTION

I am often asked to give parents and grandparents ideas for cakes for both their children and grandchildren. I have always enjoyed creating new cakes for children and, for this reason, it has given me great pleasure to create these thirty-two new designs.

I do feel that it is always worth finding the time needed to make and decorate a cake. Knowing that time can be a precious commodity, I have designed some cakes that are extremely quick and simple, and others that can be prepared in advance. Some could even be made by decorating a shop-bought cake as imaginative touches make the cake unique to the child for whom it is intended.

This book opens with a selection of tried and tested recipes for making the basic cakes, coatings and modelling paste. All the designs stipulate whether they are intended for sponge or fruit cakes, and many are suitable for either according to individual taste. Most younger children prefer the lighter sponge cake but older children, particularly teenagers, may well enjoy the richer taste of fruit cake.

The designs include easy-to-learn decorating techniques such as cut-out shapes and modelling in sugarpaste, chocolate and almond paste; runouts and plaques in royal icing; and an ingenious use of meringue. (All of these techniques are shown in the step-by-step instructions and beginners should also refer to the glossary at the end of the book). I have also used everyday items from the supermarket such as sweets, biscuits and candied fruits to save time and add the finishing touches.

The cakes have been arranged according to age, although many of the ideas will delight a teenager just as much as a younger child. There are designs for

boys and for girls, and some suitable for either which would also appeal to adults. Apart from the detailed, step-by-step photographs and instructions for creating the cakes, suggestions are also included as to how the design could be varied or adapted to a different age. The age of child to whom the cake would appeal and, where appropriate, other possible occasions for use, are also indicated. Some of the designs are simple enough for children to help with, and teenagers could well enjoy creating a cake as a surprise for mum or dad – or a younger brother or sister.

All of the designs leave scope for using your own imagination and can be adapted in content or colour. The 'Birthday Wishes' cake on page 64, for instance, can easily be varied in colour or in the items placed around the cake, which could incorporate models of treasured possessions, and be linked to special interests or hobbies.

Similarly, once the basic technique has been mastered, almost any shape can be cut out, coated and decorated. The nursery rhyme cakes could feature old favourites such as Humpty Dumpty, or characters from contemporary cartoons or favourite stories.

Some of the sugarpaste decorations are suitable for giving to party guests as gifts to take home, whilst the 'Christmas Cracker' on page 94 has individual cakes around it with each child's name on them. This original idea could easily be adapted for a table setting, so that each child has his/her own cake place-marker to take home.

I hope that this book will provide inspiration and fire your enthusiasm for decorating children's cakes, and that you and your children will have hours of fun and pleasure from these new designs.

ALL-IN-ONE-SPONGE

INGREDIENTS

Self-raising flour	170g (6oz)
Baking powder	1½ level teaspoons
Soft margarine	170g (6oz)
Caster sugar	170g (6oz)
Eggs	(size 3) 3

Bake at 170°C (325°F) or gas mark 3 for approximately 30 minutes.

VARIATIONS

For a chocolate sponge, use 30g (1oz) cocoa powder to 145g (5oz) of flour.

ITEMS REQUIRED

2 round sponge tins	20.5cm (8")
Greaseproof paper	
Wire cooling tray	

STORING

The sponge may be wrapped in waxed paper and deep-frozen for up to 6 months. Use within 3 days of baking or after defrosting.

1

Heat the oven to the recommended temperature. Grease both tins with white fat and line the bases with greased greaseproof paper.

2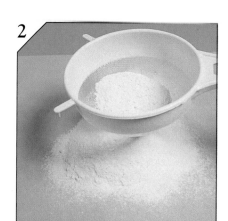

Sieve the flour and baking powder three times to ensure a fine consistency.

3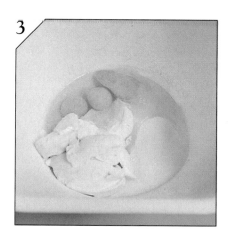

Place all the ingredients together in a mixing bowl.

4

Beat the ingredients together for 3-4 minutes, until thoroughly mixed and of a light consistency.

5

Divide mixture evenly between the 2 greased and lined tins. Bake the sponges in pre-heated oven for approximately 30 minutes. Test before removing (see p.7).

6

After baking, leave the sponges in the tins for 5 minutes before turning out on to a wire cooling tray.

LIGHT SPONGE

INGREDIENTS

Eggs	170g (6oz)
Caster sugar	170g (6oz)
Hot water	85g (3oz)
Self-raising flour	170g (6oz)

Bake at 200°C (400°F) or gas mark 6 for approximately 14 minutes.

ITEMS REQUIRED

Two round
sponge tins   20.5cm (8")
Wire cooling tray

STORING

The sponge may be wrapped in waxed paper and deep-frozen for up to 6 months. Use within 3 days of baking or after defrosting.

SPONGE BAKING TEST

Bake the sponge for the recommended time, or until golden brown. Test by pressing the surface lightly with finger tips. If this leaves an indentation, continue baking. Repeat test every 2-3 minutes until the surface springs back when touched.

1 Grease the 2 tins with white fat and sprinkle with sufficient flour to cover the base and sides. Tap out excess flour.

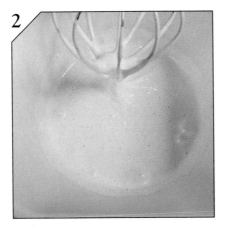

2 Place the eggs and sugar in a mixing bowl and whisk together well until thick and creamy.

3 Pour in the hot water and stir into the egg and sugar mixture.

4 Sieve the flour and gently fold it into the mixture using a spatula.

5 Divide mixture evenly between the 2 greased tins. Bake the sponges near the top of a pre-heated oven for 14 minutes. Test before removing (see above).

6 After baking, leave the sponges in the tins for 5 minutes before turning out onto a wire cooling tray.

GENOESE SPONGE

INGREDIENTS

Butter	85g (3oz)
Margarine	85g (3oz)
Caster sugar	170g (6oz)
Eggs	170g (6oz)
Self-raising flour	170g (6oz)

Bake at 180°C (350°F) or gas mark 4 for approximately 22 minutes.

ITEMS REQUIRED

2 round sponge tins   20.5cm (8")
Greaseproof paper
Wire cooling tray

STORING
The sponge may be wrapped in waxed paper and deep-frozen for up to 6 months. Use within 3 days of baking or after defrosting.

1 Heat the oven to the recommended temperature. Grease the inside of the tins with white fat and line the base with greased greaseproof paper.

2 Place the butter, margarine and sugar in a mixing bowl and beat together until light.

3 Lightly mix the eggs together and gradually add them to the mixture, beating thoroughly until all the egg is used.

4 Add the flour and, using a spatula, gently fold it into the mixture. Do not over-mix.

5 Put mixture into prepared tins and spread evenly with a spatula. Bake in the centre of pre-heated oven for approximately 22 minutes. Test before removing (see p.7).

6 After baking, leave sponge in tin for 5 minutes before turning out onto a wire cooling tray.

CHOCOLATE SPONGE

INGREDIENTS

Butter	225g (8oz)
Caster sugar	225g (8oz)
Eggs	(size 3), separated 6
Plain flour	170g (6oz)
Cocoa powder	60g (2oz)
Baking powder	2 teaspoons
Pinch of salt	

Bake at 200°C (400°F) or gas mark 6 for approximately 20 minutes.

ITEMS REQUIRED

Two round greased sponge tins	20.5cm (8")
Wire cooling tray	

STORING
The cake may be wrapped in waxed paper and deep-frozen for up to 6 months. Use within 3 days of baking or after defrosting.

1 Heat the oven to the recommended temperature. Place the fat and sugar in a bowl and cream together.

2 Add the egg yolks a little at a time and beat into the creamed mixture.

3 Sieve together the flour, cocoa and baking powder and beat well into the creamed mixture.

4 Whisk the egg whites until they are firm and gently fold them into the cake mixture.

5 Divide the mixture evenly between the 2 greased tins and bake in the centre of the pre-heated oven for 20 minutes. Test before removing (see p.7).

6 After baking, leave the cake in the tins for 5 minutes before turning out onto a wire cooling tray.

SWISS ROLL

INGREDIENTS

Eggs	(size 3) 2
Caster sugar	75g (2½oz)
Warm water	1 teaspoon
Plain flour	60g (2oz)

For a chocolate Swiss roll, use 45g (1½oz) plain flour with 15g (½oz) cocoa powder.

Bake at 220°C (425°F) or gas mark 7 for approximately 7-8 minutes.

ITEMS REQUIRED

Swiss roll tin	29cm x 19cm
	(11½" x 7½")

Greaseproof paper

STORING
The Swiss roll may be wrapped in waxed paper and deep-frozen for up to 6 months. Use within 3 days of baking or after defrosting.

1

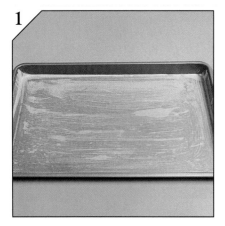

Heat the oven to the recommended temperature. Grease the Swiss roll tin and line the base and shorter sides with greased greaseproof paper.

2

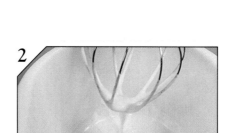

Whisk the eggs and sugar together in a bowl until the mixture is thick and creamy.

3

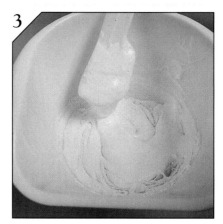

Stir in the warm water. Sieve the flour (and cocoa powder, if making a chocolate Swiss roll) and gently fold it into the mixture.

4

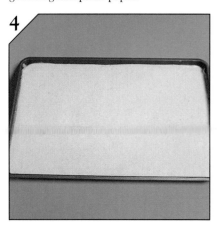

Spread mixture into prepared Swiss roll tin and level the surface. Bake at 220°C (425°F), gas mark 7, for approximately 7-8 minutes. Test before removing (see p.7).

5

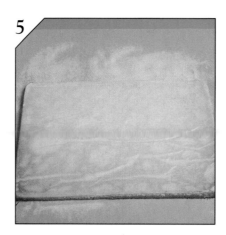

Turn out the sponge onto greaseproof paper lightly sprinkled with caster sugar. Leave to cool for 5 minutes.

6

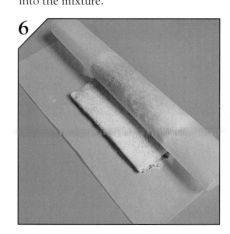

Trim edges and roll up the sponge in the greaseproof paper, starting at the short end. Keep tightly rolled until cold. Unroll, fill and re-roll to finish, as required.

LIGHT FRUIT CAKE

INGREDIENTS

Butter	170g (6oz)
Caster sugar	170g (6oz)
Ground almonds	45g (1½oz)
Egg	170g (6oz)
Self-raising flour	170g (6oz)
Cherries (halved)	130g (4½oz)
Cherries (chopped)	45g (1½oz)
Currants	130g (4½oz)
Sultanas	170g (6oz)
Mixed peel	85g (3oz)
Rum	22g (¾oz)
Lemon zest and juice	¾ lemon

NOTE: Leave all ingredients in a warm place, approximately 18°C (65°F), for 12 hours before commencing.

Bake at 170°C (325°F) or gas mark 3 for approximately 2¼ hours.

ITEMS REQUIRED

Round cake tin	20.5cm (8") or
Square cake tin	18cm (7")
Greaseproof paper	

STORING
When the cake is cold, wrap it in waxed paper and store out of direct sunlight in a cool dry place with adequate ventilation. Do not store in a sealed plastic container, cling film or foil.

1

LINING THE TIN: Grease the inside of the tin with white fat and line the base and sides with greased greaseproof paper.

2
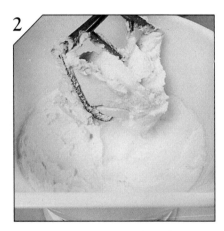
MAKING THE CAKE: Heat the oven to the recommended temperature. Beat the butter and sugar until light, and stir in the ground almonds.

3

Lightly mix the eggs together and gradually add them to the mixture, beating thoroughly until all the egg is used. Fold in the sieved flour to form a batter.

4

Mix together all the fruit, rum, lemon zest and juice and stir into the batter. Ensure that all the fruit is evenly dispersed.

5

Transfer the mixture to the prepared tin and level the surface. Bake in the centre of the oven for approximately 2¼ hours.

6

BAKING TEST: Insert skewer into cake centre and withdraw carefully. If skewer remains clean the cake is baked, if sticky, continue until baked.

SUGARPASTE

INGREDIENTS

Water	2 tablespoons
Powdered gelatine	1½ level teaspoons
Liquid glucose	1½ tablespoons
Glycerine	2 teaspoons
Icing sugar (sieved)	455g (16oz)

Sugarpaste is a firm, sweet paste which can be made in advance and kept in a polythene bag in a refrigerator for up to two weeks (the bag should be labelled with the date it was made).

Food colourings can be kneaded into the paste, but care should be taken that sufficient quantity is coloured to complete the project, as it is difficult to match colours at a later date. Sugarpaste can also be coloured by painting food colourings on afterwards, once the paste is dry.

Sugarpaste is ideal for covering cakes as it can be easily rolled out on a board dusted with icing sugar.

Decorations for cakes can be made by cutting shapes from rolled out paste.

Sugarpaste is easily shaped with fingers, and therefore animals, figures and flowers can be hand-modelled and used to make attractive decorations.

MAKING SUGARPASTE: Pour the water into a stainless steel or non-stick saucepan. Sprinkle on powdered gelatine and dissolve over low heat.

Stir in glucose and glycerine and then remove the saucepan from the heat.

Gradually add the icing sugar, mixing continuously to avoid lumps developing.

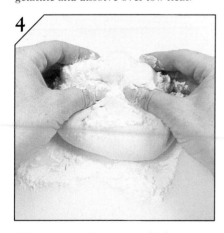

When mixture becomes a thick paste, remove from pan and place on a smooth surface. Add remaining icing sugar by kneading between fingers and thumbs. Store in labelled polythene bag until required.

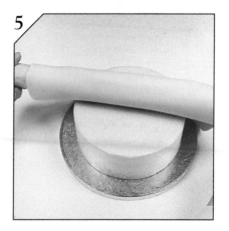

COVERING A SPONGE: Spread buttercream over the sponge. Chill for 1 hour. Lift the rolled sugarpaste with a rolling pin and lay over cake. Smooth to expel air and trim. Leave for 24 hours.

COVERING A FRUIT CAKE: Cover cake with almond paste. Brush top and sides with cooled boiled water. Lift sugarpaste with a rolling pin and lay over cake. Smooth to expel air, trim and leave for 24 hours.

BUTTERCREAM

INGREDIENTS
Butter	170g (6oz)
Icing sugar	340g (12oz)
Warm water	3 tablespoons

NOTE: All ingredients should be approximately 18°C (65°F).

CHOCOLATE BUTTERCREAM: Melt 60g (2oz) of compound or couverture chocolate in a heat-proof bowl over a pan of hot water. When the chocolate reaches 38°C (100°F), immediately beat it into 225g (8oz) of buttercream.

Soften the butter and beat until light.

Sieve the icing sugar and gradually add it to the butter, beating well after each addition. Beat in the warm water.

Colouring and flavouring may be added if required. For chocolate buttercream, beat in the melted chocolate, as shown.

ALMOND PASTE

INGREDIENTS
Caster sugar	170g (6oz)
Icing sugar	170g (6oz)
Ground almonds	340g (12oz)
Glucose syrup	225g (8oz)

TO COVER A ROUND OR SQUARE CAKE WITH ALMOND PASTE: Roll out, and cut, almond paste to fit the cake-top and fix with boiling apricot purée. Then roll out, and cut into strip(s), sufficient almond paste to cover the side(s) and fix to the cake with boiling apricot purée. Leave to dry. (If rounded edges are required, cover the whole cake in one piece of almond paste.) The cake can then be covered in sugarpaste (see p.12) or coated in two layers of soft cutting royal icing.

Sieve the icing sugar into a bowl. Add the caster sugar and ground almonds and mix.

Warm the glucose syrup and add it to the dry ingredients in the bowl.

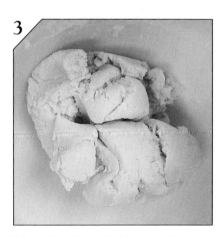

Mix well to form a pliable paste. Store in a sealed container until required. Note: The consistency of the paste can be altered by adjusting the amount of glucose.

ALBUMEN SOLUTION

INGREDIENTS

Water   170g (6oz)
Pure albumen powder 30g (1oz)

1

Pour the water into a bowl. Sprinkle the dried albumen powder into the water whilst stirring with a whisk.

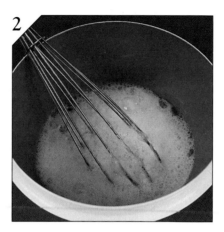

2

Thoroughly mix the albumen powder into the water. Leave for one hour, stirring occasionally.

3

Strain the mixture through a sieve or muslin. It is then ready for use.

ROYAL ICING

INGREDIENTS

Fresh egg whites or
albumen solution   85g (3oz)

Icing sugar or
confectioners' sugar
(sieved)   455g (16oz)

NOTE: If using fresh egg white, separate 24 hours before making the royal icing.

FOR SOFT-CUTTING ICING: Use 3 teaspoons of glycerine to every 455g (16oz) of royal icing.

N.B.: Glycerine should only be added after the royal icing has been made. It should not be added for runouts or No. 1 work.

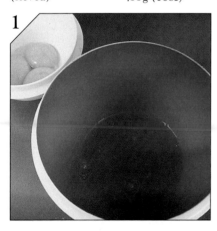

1

Place the fresh egg whites or albumen solution into a bowl.

2

Stir one-third of the icing sugar into the egg white or albumen solution and beat well. Repeat until all the icing sugar has been added.

3

Beat the mixture until light and fluffy and peaks can be formed. Scrape down the inside of the bowl and cover with a damp cloth until required.

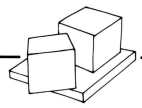

ITEMS REQUIRED

2 square sponges
    15cm x 15cm (6" x 6")

Sugarpaste
    680g (1½lb)

Jam and buttercream for filling and
    coating

Cake board
    30.5cm x 25.5cm (12" x 10")

Crimper

Assorted food colourings

Small quantity of royal icing without
    glycerine

Piping tube No.1

Round crimped cutters

Birthday candle and holder

Artificial flowers

This cake incorporates all baby's favourite items and could help with learning to talk as each item can be named prior to cutting the cake.

Although Mary created this particular cake for a one year old, the design can easily be adapted to any age simply by changing the cut-out number and figures, and using the appropriate number of candles.

An enterprising mum can easily find a multitude of suitable figures in children's story books or toy catalogues. Designs could

incorporate much loved toys, story or cartoon characters to add a particularly personal touch to the cake.

1

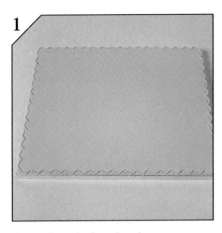

Cover the cake board with sugarpaste. Crimp the edges, as shown. Leave to dry for 12 hours.

2

Cutting and layering: Cut the 2 sponges in half horizontally and spread jam and buttercream between each layer, as shown.

3

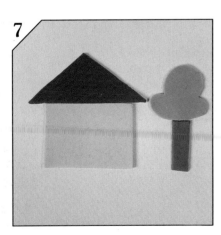

Coat sponge top and sides with buttercream. Cut pieces of sugarpaste to cover, as shown. Smooth the sugarpaste to expel any trapped air, and trim.

4

Cut sugarpaste flower shapes, using template A as a guide. Place on greaseproof paper and leave to dry.

5

Using template B as a guide, cut out sugarpaste shapes for the cat. Place on greaseproof paper and leave to dry.

6

Cut out sugarpaste shapes for the yacht, using template C as a guide. Place on greaseproof paper and leave to dry.

7

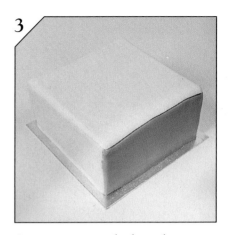

Using template D as a guide, cut out sugarpaste shapes to make the house and tree. Place on greaseproof paper and leave to dry.

8

Cut the number 1 from sugarpaste, using template E as a guide. Place on greaseproof paper and leave to dry.

9

Pipe dots of royal icing onto the centre of each flower (No.1). Decorate the flower pot by piping with royal icing (No. 1).

Pipe eyes, nose, mouth and whiskers onto the cat's face, as shown (No.1).

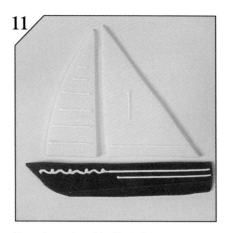

Pipe the sail and hull markings on the yacht with royal icing, as shown (No. 1).

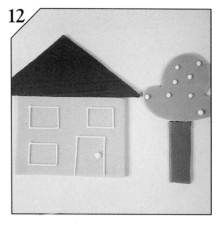

Pipe windows and a door on the house in royal icing, and pipe dots on the tree (No.1).

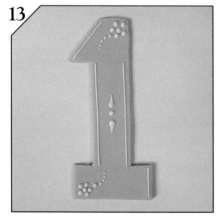

Decorate the number by piping a design in royal icing (No.1).

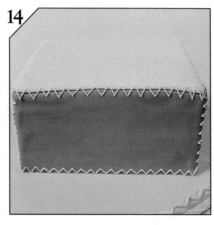

Place the building block on the covered cake board and pipe zigzags of royal icing around the cake-edges, as shown (No.1).

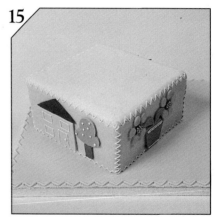

Moisten and fix the sugarpaste shapes to the cake-sides.

Fix the figure one onto the cake-top and pipe inscription in royal icing (No.1).

Complete the piped inscription (No.1), as shown.

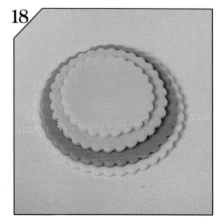

Cut circles of sugarpaste in varying colours and sizes. Moisten and fix to the board with candle and holder. Add artificial flowers to complete the decoration.

A

B

C

TEMPLATES

D

E

ITEMS REQUIRED

Round sponge cake
   25.5cm (10")
Sugarpaste
   680g (1½lb)
Assorted food colourings
Jam and buttercream for filling and
   coating
Small quantity of royal icing
Round cake board
   33cm (13")
Crimper
Piping tube No's. 0 and 13
2 round crimped cutters
   7cm (2¾") and 4.5cm (1¾") in
   diameter
Length of ribbon
   1cm (½") wide

This appealing cake is ideal for helping a toddler to learn nursery rhymes - and for mum to practise her skills at writing in icing!

The template makes cutting out the horse's head a simple task but an imaginative mum could also use the technique to create other favourite nursery rhyme characters such as baa-baa black sheep.

Templates can easily be created from the drawings in a storybook. If a larger cake is required, the template can quickly be increased in size by the use of an enlarging photocopier.

The head is decorated with an effective combination of piped royal icing and sugarpaste cut-outs with artificial ribbon to provide the finishing touch.

This cake is ideal for young children aged 1-4 but could also be adapted for teenagers who enjoy horse riding.

1

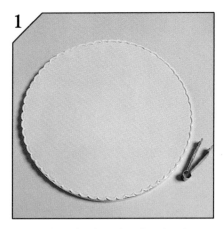

Cover the cake board with a thin layer of sugarpaste. Crimp the edges. Leave to dry for 12 hours.

2

Cut the sponge to shape, using the template as a guide. Cut and layer the sponge, then coat top and sides with buttercream.

3

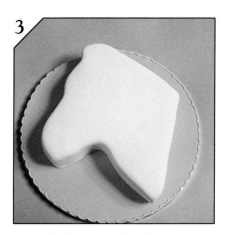

Cover the horse's head with sugarpaste, as shown (see p.12) and place it on the covered board.

4

Cut sugarpaste shapes for the bridle. Moisten and fix to the head.

5

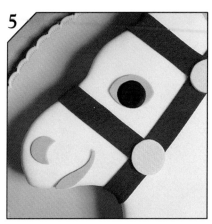

Cut sugarpaste shapes for the eye, nostril and mouth. Moisten and fix to the head, as shown.

6

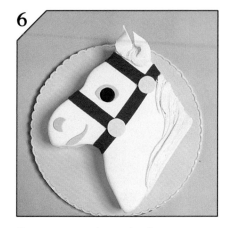

Cut sugarpaste shapes for the ears. Moisten and fix to the head, as shown. Pipe the horse's mane in royal icing (No.13).

7

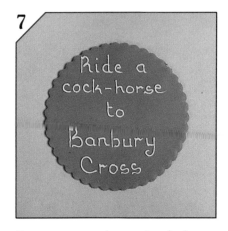

Cut a sugarpaste plaque using the large round crimped cutter. Pipe inscription of choice in royal icing (No. 0).

8

Cut another plaque using the smaller cutter and pipe inscription of choice in royal icing (No. 0).

9

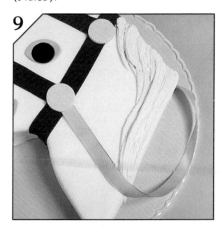

Make reins from the length of ribbon and fix into position with a little royal icing. Fix the plaques in the same way.

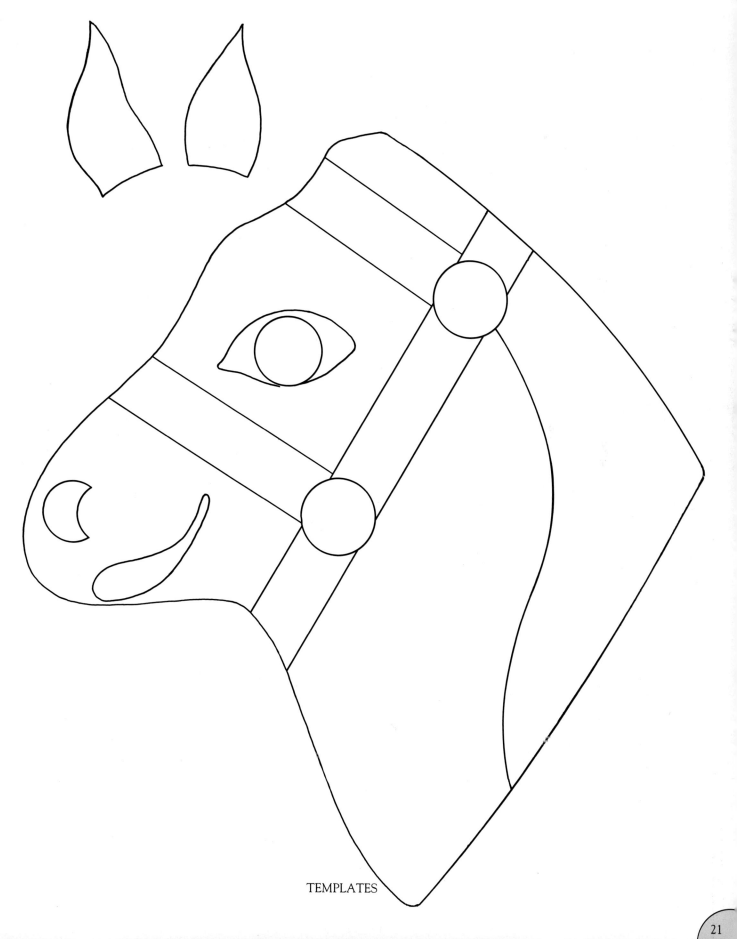

TEMPLATES

TRAIN

ITEMS REQUIRED

2 sponges
    29cm x 19cm (11½" x 7½")
Jam and buttercream for filling and
    coating
Sugarpaste
    340g (12oz)
Assorted food colourings
Nibbed almonds, toasted
    85g (3oz)
3 chocolate-coated biscuits
    7cm (2¾") diameter
Royal icing
    115g (4oz)
Cake board
    40.5cm x 30.5cm (16" x 12")
Piping tube No's. 1, 2 and 3

Trains, a perennial favourite with
young boys, are an ideal subject for
cakes.

This striking design provides an
extremely good example of how to
shape a sponge cake, and it can be
adapted to make other shapes as
required.

This cake also demonstrates how to
use materials which are usually in
the kitchen, such as biscuits.

Mary piped onto chocolate biscuits
with royal icing to make the train
wheels.

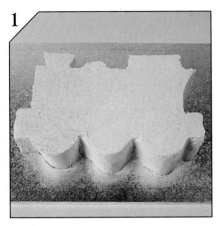

1 Layer the sponges (see step 2 on p.15) and cut to the shape shown, using the template as a guide. Coat the top and sides with buttercream.

2 Cut out the sugarpaste shape shown using template A and fix into position.

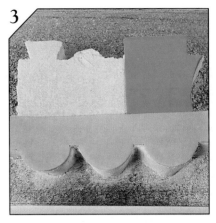

3 Cut out the sugarpaste shape shown using template B and fix into position.

4 Cut out the sugarpaste shape shown using template C and fix into position.

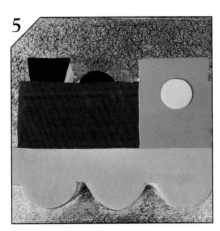

5 Cut out the sugarpaste shapes shown using templates D, E and F and fix into position.

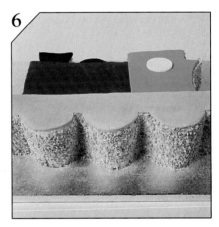

6 Cover the sides of the sponge with the toasted nibbed almonds.

7 Pipe wheel detail in royal icing onto the chocolate biscuits, as shown (No.3). Make wheel centres from sugarpaste and fix wheels to train with royal icing.

8 Pipe detail onto the rest of the train using coloured royal icing (No.2).

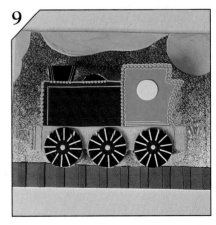

9 Cut out sugarpaste shapes for the track and sky. Fix to the board with royal icing. Pipe the inscription in royal icing (No.1).

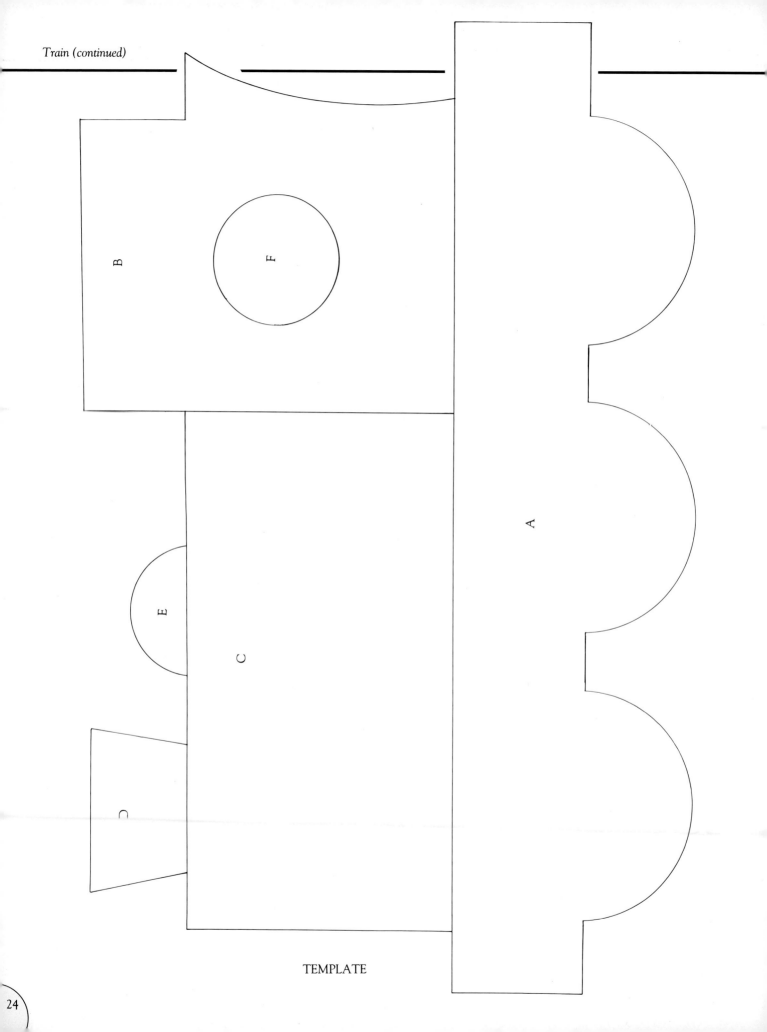

TEMPLATE

TELEPHONE

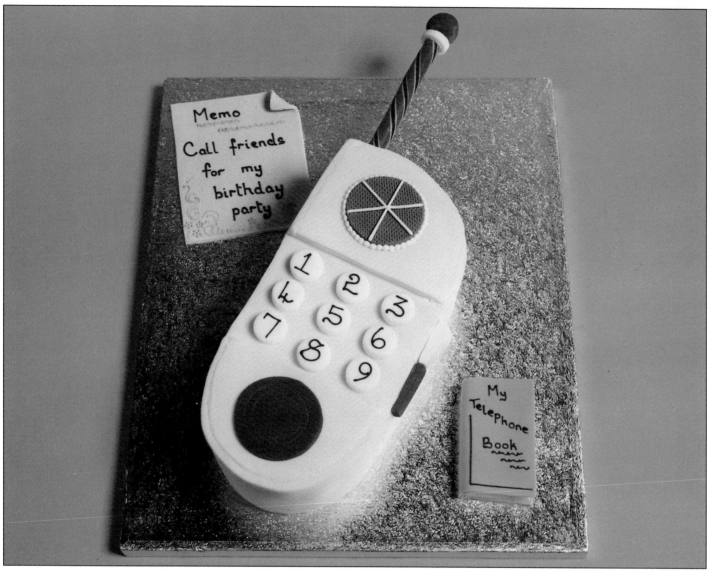

ITEMS REQUIRED

Sponge made in a 680g (1½lb)
    loaf tin

Jam and buttercream for filling and
    coating

Sugarpaste
    455g (16oz)

Assorted food colourings

Small quantity of royal icing

Small, thin stick of rock

Loaf tin 680g (1½lb)
Rectangular cake board
    25.5cm x 30.5cm (10" x 12")

Large and small round cutters

Piping tubes No's. 0, 1 and 2

All young children are fascinated by
the telephone and this cake presents
them with one of their very own
as well as giving a strong hint to
teenagers who often spend most of
their time on the phone!

It is an up-to-the minute cordless
model, cunningly utilising a stick of
rock for the aerial, and it comes
complete with its own accessories
of memo pad and telephone book.

The cake is easily adapted for any
age, and the age could be
emphasised by highlighting the

appropriate number in a different
colour.

The message on the memo pad
could also be personalised or
changed to suit the occasion.

1

Bake a sponge in a 680g (1½lb) loaf tin using 340g (12oz) of genoese batter. Leave to cool on a wire tray.

2

Using a sharp knife, cut and trim the sponge to the shape shown.

3

Cut and layer the sponge (see step 2 on p.15) and coat top and sides with buttercream. Cut end shapes from thick sugarpaste and position as shown.

4

Cover sides and centre panel with thinly rolled sugarpaste, as shown.

5

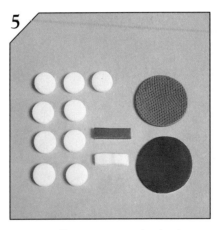

Cut 9 small sugarpaste circles for digits and 2 large circles for end pieces. Cut 2 oblongs for side switches. Leave to dry.

6

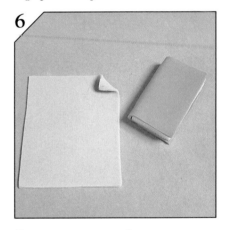

Cut sugarpaste rectangles in appropriate sizes and thicknesses to make the telephone book and memo pad, as shown.

7

Pipe digits on small circles and design on one end piece (No.1). When icing is dry, fix pieces to the telephone using a little royal icing.

8

Pipe design and wording of choice onto telephone book and memo pad (No. 0). When dry, arrange and fix the book and pad onto the cake board using royal icing.

9

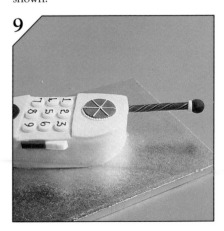

Make an aerial by fixing a small sugarpaste ball to the end of the rock. Push the rock into the telephone, as shown. Fix side switch to cake with royal icing.

SPEEDY THE TURTLE

ITEMS REQUIRED

2 sponges
Jam and buttercream for filling and
    coating
Sugarpaste
    570g (1¼lb)
Assorted food colourings
Small quantity of royal icing
Oven-proof pudding basin
    285g (½ pint)
Pyrex dish
    800ml (1½ pint)
Oval cake board
    25.5cm x 30.5cm (10" x 12")
Piping tube No's. 1, 2 and 7
Silk flower
Cake candles and holders

This delightful cake demonstrates
how easily unusual shapes can be
created with a little imagination.

Mary used a pudding basin and a
Pyrex dish to bake the sponges for
the head and the body, which she
then decorated with coloured
sugarpaste to create a cute character.

Designed to appeal to boys and girls
of all ages, Speedy could easily wear
a bonnet instead of a hat, as it is
difficult to distinguish Master from
Miss Turtle.

1 Make 2 sponges, one in the pudding basin and another in the Pyrex dish.

4 Colour the sugarpaste in a darker shade, and cut shapes for the shell markings. Moisten and fix, as shown.

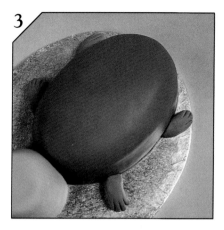

7 Make a top hat from sugarpaste, moisten and fix to the top of the head, as shown.

2 Cut and layer both sponges (see step 2 on p.15) and coat the outsides with buttercream. Cover each sponge with sugarpaste, as shown (see p.12).

5 Cut further shapes, moisten and fix to the base of the shell, covering flippers, as shown.

8 Make a hat band from a strip of sugarpaste and fix to the hat. Pipe name, or inscription of choice, onto the brim (No.1). Fix a silk flower to the top of the hat.

3 Cut out the turtle's flippers from sugarpaste. Mark each flipper with the back of a knife, moisten and fix into position.

6 Cut sugarpaste shapes for the eyes and nose, and make a roll for the mouth. Pipe the nostrils with royal icing (No. 2). Moisten features and fix to the head.

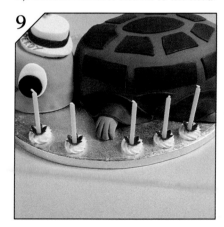

9 Pipe rosettes of royal icing (No.7) around the edge of the cake board. Fix a candle holder and candle into each rosette.

ITEMS REQUIRED

2 round chocolate sponges
    20.5cm (8")
Chocolate for roof supports
    approximately 60g (2oz)
Coconut flour
    60g (2oz)
Chocolate for roof approximately
    85g (3oz)
Buttercream for filling and coating
Sugarpaste
    455g (16oz)
Small, thin stick of rock
Royal icing
    115g (4oz)
Assorted food colourings
Oval cake board
    35.5cm x 30.5cm (14" x 12")

Fine paintbrush
Piping tube (No. 1)
Round crimped cutter
Several small bells
Pair of large bells

This appealing cake demonstrates a wide range of techniques and utilises one of children's favourite tastes, chocolate.

Although the design does need time and patience, the finished cake is well worth the effort involved and it will delight any child's heart.

Beginners should allow themselves plenty of time to complete each stage and prepare the cake when free from distractions.

A fruit cake could be used as the basis but would require coating with almond paste at stage 6 instead of coating with buttercream.

ROOF SUPPORTS: Melt the chocolate in a heat-proof bowl over hot water and then stir in the coconut flour.

Spread the chocolate and coconut mixture thickly onto silicone paper and leave to set.

Using a sharp knife, cut the two roof supports to the shape shown.

ROOF: Melt the chocolate in a bowl over hot water and spread onto silicone paper. Leave to set. Cut two rectangles measuring 14cm x 7.5cm (5½" x 3").

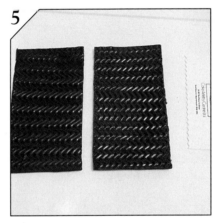

Re-melt scraps of chocolate and spread a thin layer over the roof pieces. Before it sets, pass a comb scraper over the surface to create a tile pattern.

WELL: Sandwich sponges with butter-cream and position to one side of cake board. Thinly spread remaining butter-cream over top and sides, then chill.

Cover the top and sides of the sponge with sugarpaste, overlapping the sugarpaste on the top edge, as shown.

Cut sufficient bricks from thick sugarpaste to cover outer edge. Moisten and fix, as shown. Paint brick effect on well sides using a fine paintbrush.

Mount the roof supports on the cake-top by fixing with a little melted chocolate. Fix the rock, in the same way, between the supports.

10

Fix the roof panels to the supports, using a little melted chocolate.

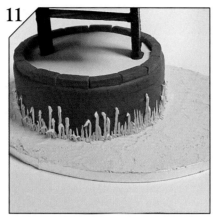

11

Coat the cake board with green royal icing, stippling to give a grass effect. Pipe blades of grass around the well sides using a leaf-shaped bag.

12

Make a cat's head and paws from sugarpaste and pipe features with royal icing. Make a handle from sugarpaste. Fix all pieces with royal icing, as shown.

13

Pipe the first two lines of the nursery rhyme onto the roof, using royal icing (No.1).

14

Pipe the third line of the nursery rhyme onto the other roof side (No. 1).

15

Cut a sugarpaste plaque using a crimped, round cutter. Decorate the plaque by piping a birthday message and flowers in royal icing (No. 1).

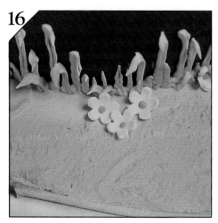

16

Make sugarpaste flowers in different sizes and pipe the centres with green royal icing (No. 1). Fix the flowers around the base of the well, using royal icing.

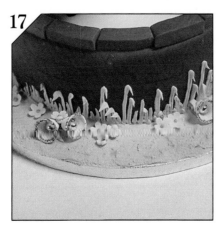

17

Fix the small bells to the iced cake board using a little royal icing.

18

Complete the cake by fixing the plaque and a pair of large bells to the iced cake board, as shown.

FORT

ITEMS REQUIRED

2 sponges made in a large Swiss roll tin,
    approximately 33cm x 23cm
    (13" x 9")

Jam and buttercream for filling and
    coating

Sugarpaste
    455g (16oz)

Royal icing
    340g (12oz)

Assorted food colourings

Square cake board
    30.5cm x 30.5cm (12" x 12")

Piping tube No's. 1, 4 and 42

Small flag

Cowboy and indian figures

Forts have always appealed to small
boys, and Mary designed this one for
those who enjoy playing cowboys
and indians.

It could however be decorated with
soldiers or, adapted to a castle, with
knights depending on where the
boy's interest lies.

Although the cake looks very
impressive, it is in fact extremely
easy to make as it utilises sugarpaste
cut-outs and piped royal icing for
the decorative detail.

This cake would be suitable for all
small boys aged from 3 to 9.

1

Layer the sponges (see step 2 on p.15) and cut into a 23cm (9") square. Cut some of the remaining sponge into 4 and coat top and sides of all pieces with buttercream.

2

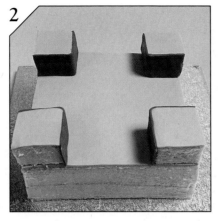

Cover cake-top with sugarpaste. Cut sugarpaste to fit the tops of each tower and assemble as shown. Cover inner sides of towers with darker sugarpaste.

3

Cover the sides of the cake with darker coloured sugarpaste as shown.

4

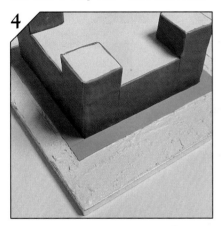

Cut narrow strips of sugarpaste and place around cake-base to make a moat. Cover the remaining cake board with royal icing and stipple with a sponge.

5

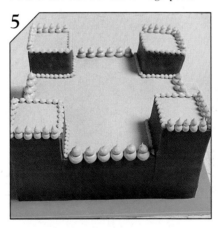

Pipe the edges of the cake-top, and around the towers, with royal icing (No. 3).

6

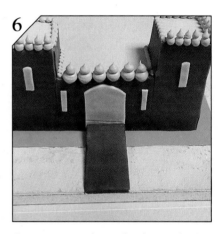

Cut sugarpaste shapes for the windows, door and drawbridge. Moisten and fix as shown.

7

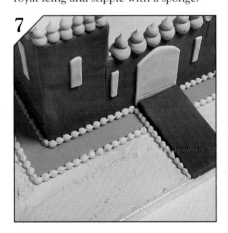

Pipe a shell border, using royal icing, around the base of the fort, drawbridge and moat (No. 42).

8

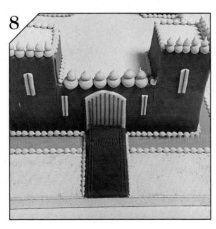

Pipe detail on the windows and drawbridge in royal icing (No. 1).

9

Pipe inscription of choice on the cake-top in royal icing (No. 1). Decorate the fort with the cowboy and indian figures, and a flag.

DOLLY DAYDREAM

ITEMS REQUIRED

Square sponge
   20.5cm x 20.5cm (8" x 8")
Jam and buttercream for filling and
   coating
Sugarpaste
   455g (16oz)
Assorted food colourings
Small quantity of royal icing
Cake board
   25.5cm x 35.5cm (10" x 14")
Piping tube No's. 1, 2 and 13
Length of narrow ribbon

This delightful cake can easily be adapted, whilst retaining the basic template, to represent a little girl's favourite doll and outfit.

The clothes are extremely easy to make, being cut out from sugarpaste and then piped with royal icing to create pattern and detail.

Although this cake is ideal for

young girls from toddlers to pre-teens, by creating a boy doll the cake could also be used for boys aged between 1 and 4.

Teenage girls would also enjoy the fun and appeal of their very own 'rag-doll' birthday cake.

1

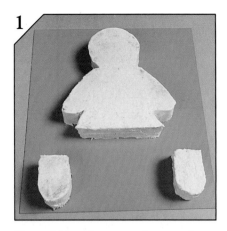

Cut and layer the sponge (see step 2 on p.15). Using the template as a guide, cut the sponge to shape and coat the top and sides with buttercream.

2

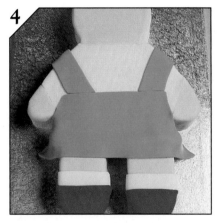

Place the doll on the cake board. Using the template as a guide, cut out shapes for the head, hands and legs from flesh coloured sugarpaste and fix.

3

Using the template as a guide, cut sugarpaste shapes for the blouse, socks and shoes and fix into place as shown.

4

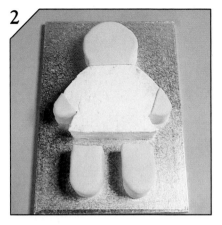

Using the template as a guide, cut sugarpaste shapes for the pinafore dress. Moisten and fix into position, as shown.

5

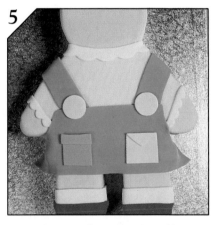

Cut sugarpaste shapes for the collar, cuffs, buttons and pockets. Moisten and fix as shown.

6

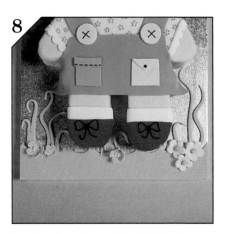

Pipe the detail on the blouse, buttons and pockets in royal icing (No. 1).

7

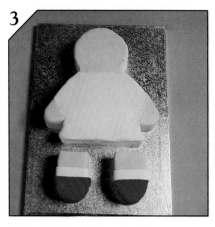

Cut circles of coloured sugarpaste for eyes. Moisten and fix to face. Pipe eyelashes (No. 1) and hair (No. 13) in royal icing. Fix a bow of ribbon to the hair.

8

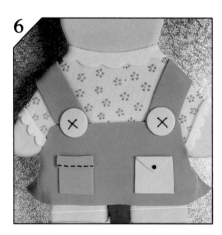

Pipe bows on shoes (No. 2). Cut lawn and blades of grass from sugarpaste and fix to board with royal icing. Make sugarpaste flowers. Moisten and fix to grass.

9

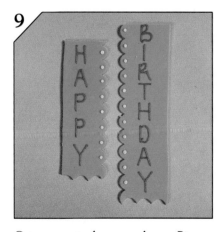

Cut sugarpaste shapes, as shown. Pipe dots and inscription of choice (No. 2) and fix to the board with royal icing.

TEMPLATE

ITEMS REQUIRED

2 sponges baked in tin measuring
     29cm x 19cm (11½" x 7½")

Sugarpaste
     570g (1¼lb)

Assorted food colourings

Jam and buttercream for filling and
     coating

Rectangular cake board
     30.5cm x 40.5cm (12" x 16")

Round cutters in 2 sizes

Royal icing
Piping tubes No's. 2 and 3

This versatile cake teaches road safety as well as being adaptable to any age - indeed, it could make an unusual and attractive eighteenth birthday cake.

Children may even enjoy helping to adapt the cake to celebrate father's birthday by drawing a template of his particular make of car and colouring and decorating it appropriately.

For older children, or adults, a fruit cake could form the basis for the cake but this would require covering with

almond paste instead of coating with buttercream in stage 3.

ROAD: Cut a sugarpaste rectangle, and fix with royal icing. Cut, moisten and fix sugarpaste 'white lines'. Pipe yellow lines in royal icing (No.3).

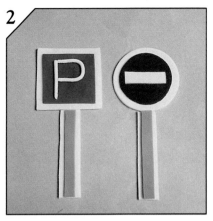

ROAD SIGNS: Cut the shapes shown in sugarpaste. Moisten and fix into position as shown.

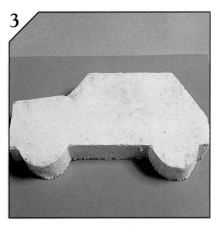

CAR: Layer the sponges (see step 2 on p.15). Using the template as a guide, cut the sponge to shape and coat the top and sides with buttercream.

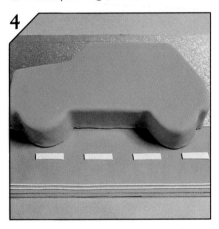

Cover the sponge with sugarpaste (see p.12) and carefully place it on the road.

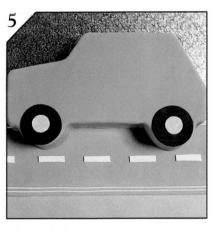

WHEELS: Cut sugarpaste wheels and hub caps. Moisten and fix to the car.

Cut 2 sugarpaste windows, door handle and filler cap. Moisten and fix to the car. Pipe detail in royal icing, as shown (No.2).

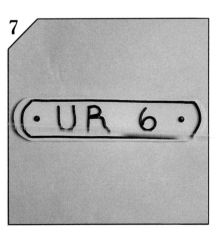

NUMBER PLATE: Cut out the number plate from sugarpaste and pipe inscription of choice with royal icing (No.1).

Make a headlight from sugarpaste. Moisten and fix to the front of the car. Fix the No Entry sign to the board using a little royal icing.

Colour a small piece of sugarpaste for the rear light. Moisten and fix to the back of the car. Fix the Parking sign to the cake board using a little royal icing.

TEMPLATE

QUACK QUACK

ITEMS REQUIRED

Round sponge
    20.5cm (8")

Round sponge
    10cm   (4")

Jam and buttercream for filling and
    coating

Sugarpaste
    455g (16oz)

Assorted food colourings

Small quantity of royal icing

Cake board
    35.5cm x 25.5cm (14" x 10")

Piping tube No. 2

Birthday candles and holders

Ducks are always popular with young children and this dapper gentleman could easily become a lady - with a little adjustment to his dress.

A parasol, bonnet and frilly skirt would soon transform Quack Quack into a suitable cake for a young lady. Or, to be really striking, he could have his hair turned into a bright green mohican.

The size of the cake is easily adjusted to suit the number of party guests.

The template can quickly be enlarged with the use of a photocopier or graph.

This cake is ideal for children aged from 1 to 7.

1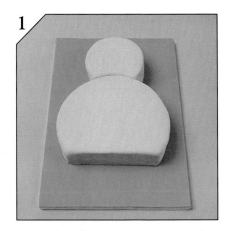

Cover the cake board in sugarpaste. Cut and layer sponges (see step 2 on p.15). Cut to shape using template as guide. Coat with buttercream and sugarpaste.

2

Using the off-cuts of sponge, cut out the feet. Spread with buttercream and cover with sugarpaste. Fix to cake board, as shown.

3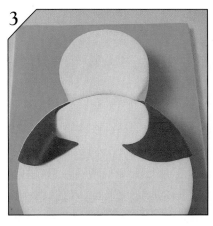

Using the template as a guide, cut sugarpaste shapes for the wings. Moisten and fix to the duck's body.

4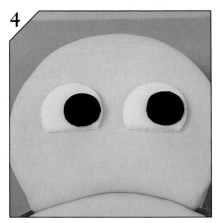

Using template as a guide, cut sugarpaste shapes for the eyes. Moisten and fix to the duck's face.

5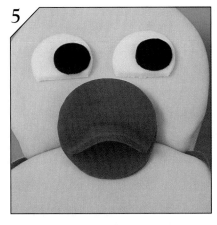

Using template as a guide, cut a sugarpaste beak. Moisten and fix, as shown.

6

Using template as a guide, cut sugarpaste head feathers. Moisten and fix to head.

7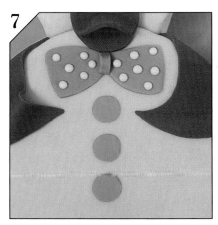

Using template as a guide, cut a sugar-paste bow tie and pipe spots in royal icing (No. 2). Cut circles of sugarpaste for the buttons. Moisten and fix.

8

Make a walking stick and blades of grass from sugarpaste. Moisten and fix, as shown.

9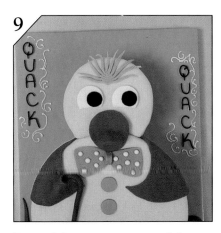

Pipe and decorate inscription of choice in royal icing (No.1). Fix birthday candles and holders onto board.

TEMPLATE

ITEMS REQUIRED

Square fruit cake
    20.5cm x 20.5cm (8" x 8")
    covered with almond paste

Sugarpaste
    570g (1¼lb)

Royal icing
    225g (8oz)

Assorted food colourings

Square cake board
    28cm x 28cm (11" x 11")

Crimper of choice

Piping tube No's. 1 and 7

This extremely effective cake is easy to make and is particularly suitable for a child who enjoys music although, with its fun character, it would be enjoyed by any youngster.

The colour can be adapted to suit a child's favourite colour and, with a little imagination, many striking colour combinations are possible.

This cake is ideal for a wide range of ages from tots to teens and could also be enjoyed by a musical adult who is still young enough at heart to enjoy the cute character.

1

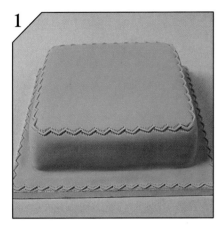

Place the almond paste covered cake (see p.11) on the board and cover cake and board with sugarpaste (see p.12). Immediately, crimp edges, as shown.

2

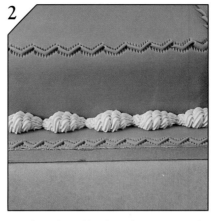

Pipe barrel scrolls of royal icing around the base of the cake (No. 7).

3

Cut out a sugarpaste music sheet. Moisten and fix to the cake-top, as shown.

4

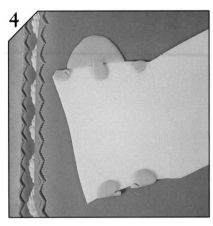

Cut out sugarpaste shapes to make the character. Moisten and fix the pieces, as shown.

5

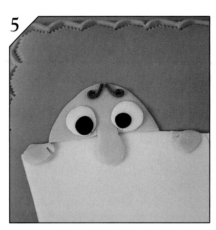

Make the eyes from sugarpaste, moisten and fix to face. Pipe 2 curls of hair on the forehead using royal icing (No. 2).

6

Pipe music notes and a message in royal icing onto one page of the music sheet (No. 1).

7

Pipe more notes and complete the message on the second page of the music sheet.

8

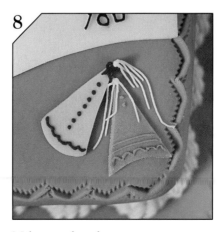

Make party hats from sugarpaste. Moisten and fix to the cake-top. Pipe the tassels in royal icing (No. 1).

9

Using sugarpaste in different colours, cut out small circles. Pipe musical notes onto each circle, moisten and fix to cake-sides. Decorate corners as required.

FIGURE FIVE

ITEMS REQUIRED

Round sponge
    18cm (7")

Square sponge
    15cm x 15cm (6" x 6")

Jam and buttercream for filling and
    coating

Wafer biscuits
    2 packets,

Compound or cooking chocolate
    115g (4oz)

Small quantity of icing sugar
Cake board
    30.5cm x 20.5cm (12" x 8")
Large and small crimped round cutters
Piping tube No's. 1 and 7
Flower and butterfly cake decorations

This striking design could be
adapted to any numeral and would
be equally suitable for a teenager's
birthday.

The textured top is quickly made
and the border around the edges is
very easily created by dipping wafer
biscuits in chocolate, so the finished
cake takes very little time to make.

Baking tins of the appropriate
numeral shape can be purchased or
hired if required or a template
prepared by copying a suitable
number.

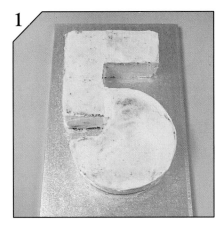

1 Cut and layer the sponges (see step 2 on p.15). Cut shapes to form a number 5. Place on cake board and coat with buttercream. Chill in a refrigerator for 1 hour.

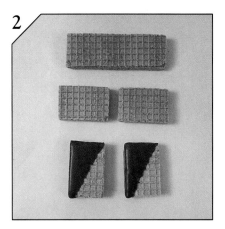

2 Melt the chocolate over a bowl of warm water. Cut each wafer biscuit in half and dip into melted chocolate, as shown. Leave to set on greaseproof paper.

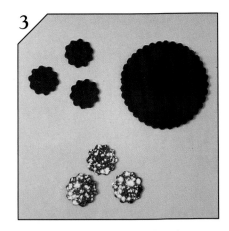

3 Spread remaining melted chocolate onto greaseproof paper. When set, cut a number of small circles and dust half with icing sugar. Cut 1 large circle.

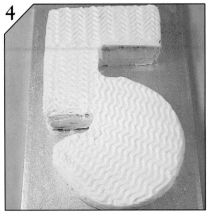

4 Coat the top of the sponge with a layer of buttercream. Comb the surface to create a pattern.

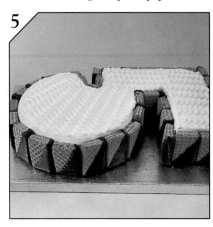

5 Fix the wafer biscuits around the edge of the sponge, arranging as shown.

6 Pipe rosettes of buttercream around the edge of the cake-top (No. 7).

7 Place the small chocolate cut-outs between the iced rosettes, alternating the plain with those dusted with icing sugar.

8 Pipe inscription of choice onto the large chocolate cut-out (No. 1) and fix to the cake-top.

9 Add further decorations as required. Pipe rosettes of buttercream onto the cake board (No. 7) and fix birthday candles and holders, as shown.

SEVEN TODAY

ITEMS REQUIRED

Round fruit cake
    20.5cm (8")
    covered with almond paste

Sugarpaste
    680g (1½lb)

Royal icing
    115g (4oz)

Assorted food colourings

Round cake board
    28cm (11")

2 crimpers in different sizes

Piping tube No's. 1, 2, 42 and 43

This attractive cake is easy to make and can be adapted for any age by tracing an appropriate numeral to make a template.

It can be made with a sponge or fruit cake.

By varing the colour, the cake is suitable for boys or girls.

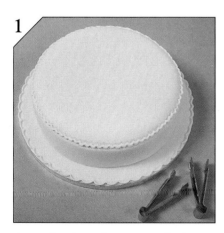

Cover the almond paste coated cake (see p.12) and the cake board with the sugarpaste (see p.10). Immediately crimp the edges.

Using the template as a guide, cut out a figure 7 from sugarpaste, moisten and fix to the cake-top. Pipe shells of royal icing around the number (No. 42).

Pipe decoration on the figure 7 in royal icing, as shown (No. 1).

47

4

Pipe grass and rabbit motifs onto the cake-top in royal icing (No. 2).

5

Begin to pipe and decorate inscription of choice in royal icing above the number 7 (No. 1).

6

Complete the piped inscription and decoration underneath the number 7.

7

Pipe a shell border in royal icing around the cake-base (No. 43).

8

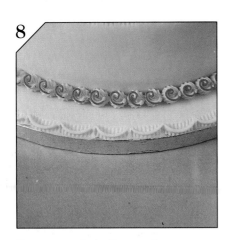

Overpipe each shell in royal icing, as shown (No. 2) and then overpipe again (No. 1).

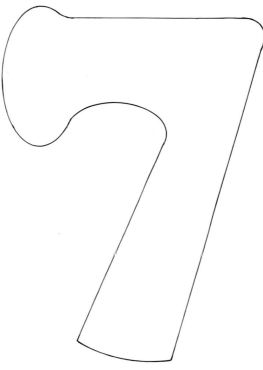

9

Pipe flower and leaf motifs in royal icing around the edge of the cake board (No. 1).

ROBBIE ROBOT

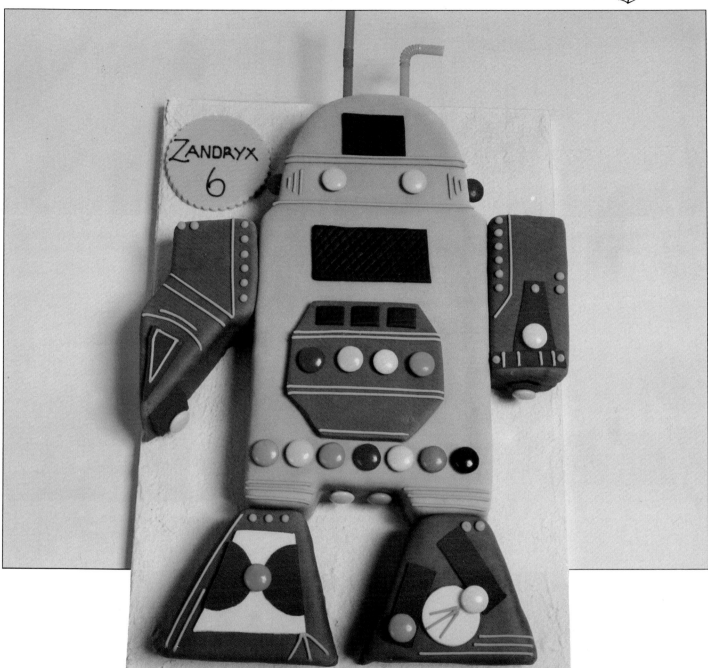

ITEMS REQUIRED

Square sponge
    20.5cm x 20.5cm (8" x 8")

Jam and buttercream for filling and
    coating

Sugarpaste
    455g (16oz)

Assorted food colourings

Smarties

Small quantity of royal icing

Rectangular cake board
    35.5cm x 25.5cm (14" x 10")

Piping tube No's. 1, 2 and 3

2 drinking straws

This ingenious cake is very easy to
make as it uses everyday items such
as Smarties and drinking straws to
achieve the colourful effect.

The cake can be made to any size

according to the number of party
guests, and the template is easily
enlarged on a photocopier or by the
use of a graph.

The colour and design on the cake
could be varied to represent a
favourite toy robot.

This cake is particularly suitable for
boys from the ages of 3 to 10.

1

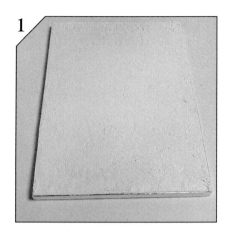

Lightly coat the cake board with coloured royal icing and stipple with a fine sponge. Leave to dry for 24 hours.

2

Using the template as a guide, cut out shapes from the sponge to make the robot, as shown.

3

Cut and layer the sponge (see step 2 on p.15) and coat cake top and sides with buttercream.

4

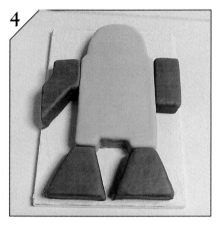

Cover all the robot pieces with sugarpaste and assemble the robot on the cake board.

5

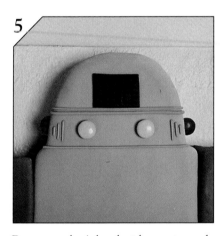

Decorate robot's head with a moistened rectangle of sugarpaste. Fix the Smarties in place and pipe lines of royal icing, as shown (No's. 2 and 3).

6

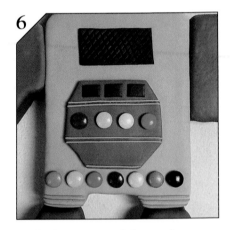

Fix further moistened shapes of sugarpaste to the body of the robot. Decorate with more Smarties and lines of piped royal icing (No. 2).

7

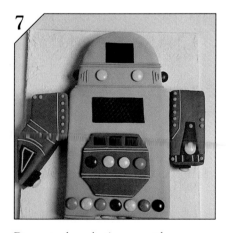

Decorate the robot's arms with sugarpaste shapes, Smarties and lines of piped royal icing as shown.

8

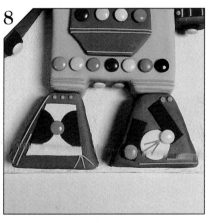

Decorate the robot's feet in a similar way, as shown.

9

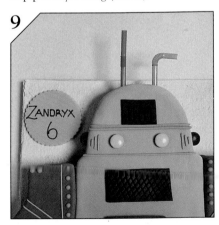

Complete the robot by piping inscription of choice on to a sugarpaste plaque. Leave to dry and fix to cake board with royal icing. Insert drinking straws antennae.

TEMPLATE

INGREDIENTS FOR
MERINGUE ROOF

Egg whites 3
Pinch of salt
Raspberry pink food colouring
Caster sugar
170g (6oz)

Bake at 100°C (200°F) or gas mark ¼ for approximately 2½-3 hours or until the outside is crisp and firm.

ITEMS REQUIRED FOR
MERINGUE ROOF

Round cake board
25.5cm (10")

Plastic scraper
Turntable
Baking tray
Savoy piping bag

ITEMS REQUIRED FOR
TOADSTOOL HOUSE

3 round sponges
15cm (6")
Jam and buttercream for filling and
coating
Sugarpaste
340g (12oz)

Assorted food colourings
Royal icing
115g (4oz)
Compound or cooking chocolate
115g (4oz)
Oval cake board
35.5cm x 30.5cm (14" x 12")
Piping tube No's. 1 and 2
Fine paintbrush
Pastry brush

This delightful cake will appeal to children of all ages.

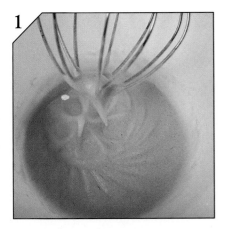

1 MERINGUE ROOF: Whisk the egg whites, salt and raspberry pink food colouring in a bowl until firm.

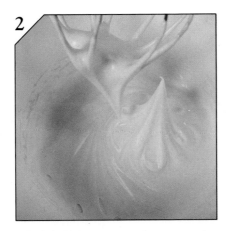

2 Whisk half the amount of sugar into the coloured egg white.

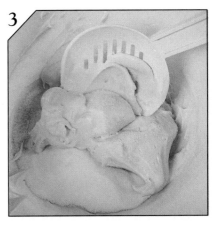

3 Gently fold the remaining half of the sugar into the mixture to form the meringue.

4 Pipe layers of meringue onto greaseproof paper placed on a board, as shown.

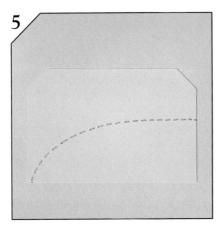

5 Cut the plastic scraper to the shape shown by the dotted line.

6 Mould meringue to shape using the shaped scraper and finish with a palette knife, using a turntable. Bake the meringue as instructed.

7 HOUSE: Layer the sponges (see step 2 on p.15). Place to one side of the cake board and coat the cake-top and sides with buttercream.

8 Cut a strip of sugarpaste to fit round the cake-side and fix, as shown.

9 Cut sugarpaste windows and door. Moisten and fix to the cake-side.

10

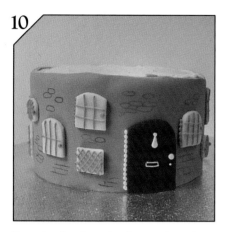

Pipe the detail on the door and windows in royal icing (No. 1). Paint the brickwork in edible food colouring using a fine paintbrush.

11

Cut a sugarpaste path. Moisten and fix to the cake board. Pipe paving design in royal icing (No. 1).

12

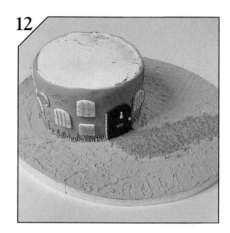

Cover remaining cake board with royal icing and stipple to give a grass effect. Pipe blades of grass around the base of the sponge (No. 2).

13

Take the prepared meringue roof and carefully scoop out the centre, as shown.

14

Melt the chocolate over a pan of warm water. Brush the melted chocolate around the inside of the meringue shell. Leave to set.

15

Fix the meringue to the cake-top to form the toadstool. Pipe inscription of choice on the top of the meringue (No. 2).

16

Cut out small circles of red sugarpaste and fix to the top of the toadstool, as shown.

17

Make a number of toadstools from sugarpaste, in various sizes. Pipe the dots in royal icing (No. 1).

18

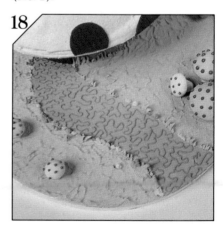

Fix the sugarpaste toadstools to the grass with a little royal icing. Pipe flowers along the path (No. 2).

ARABELLA SPIDER

ITEMS REQUIRED

Sponge made in a 1 litre (2 pint)
    pudding basin

Sugarpaste
    ~~455g~~ (16oz)

Small quantity of royal icing

Jam and buttercream for filling and
    coating

Assorted food colourings

Liquorice sticks

Round cake board
    33cm (13")

2 drinking straws

Piping tube No's. 1, 2 and 3

This cake is ideal for both birthday
and Halloween parties, and would
appeal to teenagers as well as to
young children.

The ingenious use of straws and
liquorice sticks means that Arabella
is extremely easy to make and her
impact is enhanced by the realistic
texture of her hairy body - quickly
achieved by piping with royal icing.

The cake can easily be adapted in
size by baking in a larger pudding
basin and placing on a board of the
appropriate size.

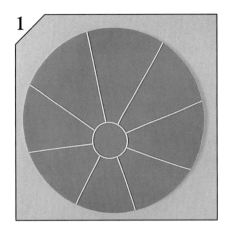

1 Cover the board in a thin layer of sugarpaste and leave to dry for 24 hours. Pipe a circle of royal icing for the centre of the cobweb then pipe the lines (No. 3).

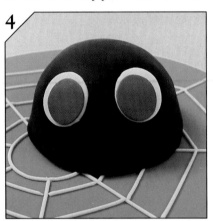

2 Complete the cobweb by piping the remaining lines in royal icing (No. 3).

3 Cut and layer the sponge (see step 2 on p.15) and coat with buttercream. Cover with sugarpaste (see p.12) and position on the cake board.

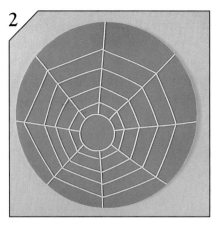

4 Make the spider's eyes from sugarpaste. Moisten and fix.

5 Make a mouth from sugarpaste. Moisten and fix. Pipe nostrils in royal icing (No. 2).

6 Pipe two-thirds of the spider's body in dark royal icing to represent hair (No. 2).

7 To make antennae, cut 2 drinking straws to the required length. Fix a ball of sugarpaste to the end of each straw and push into the top of the spider's head.

8 Bend 8 liquorice sticks and push 4 into each side of the spider's body to form the legs.

9 Pipe inscription of choice in royal icing onto cake board (No. 1).

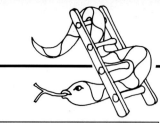

ITEMS REQUIRED

Square sponge
   30.5cm x 30.5cm (12" x 12")

Jam and buttercream for filling and
   coating

Nibbed almonds
   115g (4oz)

Sugarpaste
   340g (12oz)

Assorted food colourings

Small quantity of royal icing

Cake board
   40.5cm x 35.5cm (16" x 14")

Piping tube No's. 0, 2 and 6

Snakes and ladders is a perenniel favourite and creates a very colourful cake for any kind of children's celebration. Its universal appeal means that the design is suitable for any age or sex.

Although the design is intricate and takes a little time to assemble, it is not difficult to achieve.

Children would probably enjoy moulding the snakes and the dice themselves and would enjoy feeling that they had contributed to their brother or sister's cake.

1

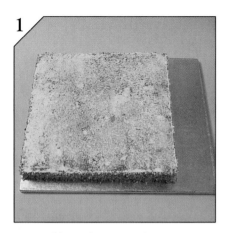

Cut and layer the sponge (see step 2 on p.15) and place on the cake board. Coat with buttercream and cover the sides with nibbed almonds.

2

Roll out sugarpaste in 4 colours and cut into 2.5cm (1") squares from each colour required. Leave all pieces to dry for 12 hours.

3

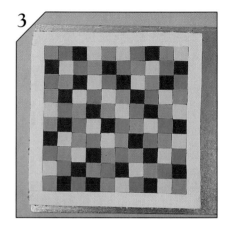

Carefully fix the squares to the cake-top. Cut and fix a sugarpaste border.

4

Pipe the ladders onto the squares in royal icing (No. 3).

5

Make sugarpaste snakes in a variety of colours and sizes. Moisten and fix to the squares, as shown.

6

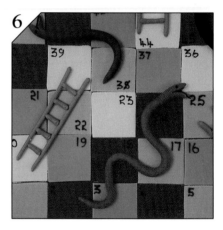

Pipe numbers on each square in royal icing (No. 0).

7

Make the counters, and a dice, from sugarpaste. Pipe dots onto dice in royal icing (No. 0). Place the pieces on the cake board.

8

Pipe inscription of choice onto cake board in royal icing (No. 2). Add decorations if required.

9

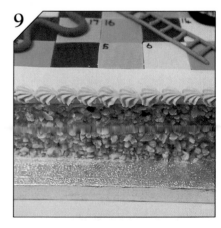

Pipe shells of royal icing around the edge of the cake-top (No. 6).

OVER THE RAINBOW

ITEMS REQUIRED

Round sponge
  20.5cm (8")

Jam and buttercream for filling and
  coating

Sugarpaste
  340g (12oz)

Assorted food colourings

Royal icing
  225g (8oz)

Round cake board
  28cm (11")

Doyley

Piping tube No's. 1 and 7

NOTE: Royal icing without glycerine
should be used for runout and No. 1
work.

This delightful cake has been
created to appeal to young ladies of
all ages but teenagers might also
enjoy making the cake as a surprise
birthday or anniversary cake for
mum.

1

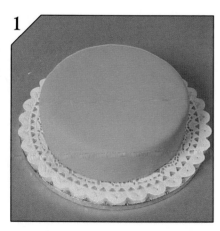

Cut and layer the sponge (see step 2 on
p.15) and coat with buttercream. Cover
the sponge with sugarpaste (see p.12).
Place on cake board with doyley.

2

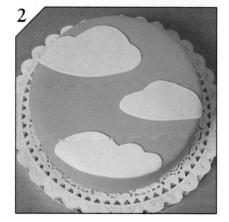

Cut sugarpaste shapes for the clouds.
Moisten and fix the clouds to the
cake-top.

3

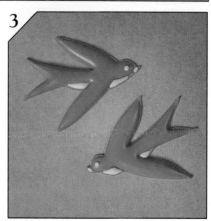

Using the template as a guide, outline
and fill in 2 bluebirds in royal icing onto
waxed paper (No. 1). Leave to dry for
24 hours.

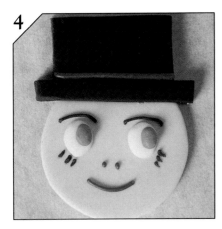

4 Using the template as a guide, cut sugarpaste shapes to make the man's face and hat. Pipe detail in royal icing (No. 1).

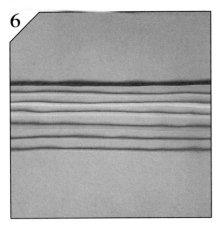

6 Colour sugarpaste in 7 different colours. Roll out into narrow strips. Place together and roll flat to form the rainbow.

8 Pipe shells of royal icing around cake-base (No. 7).

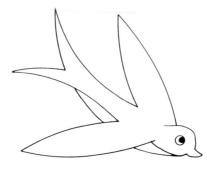

5 Using the template as a guide, cut shapes to make the lady's face and headscarf. Pipe detail in royal icing (No. 1).

7 Moisten the rainbow and fix to the cake-top, as shown.

9 Fix the birds and faces to the cake-top with royal icing. Pipe 'Over the Rainbow', or inscription of choice, in royal icing (No. 1).

ITEMS REQUIRED

2 round chocolate sponges
    25.5cm (10")
Coconut
    85g (3oz)
Green food colouring
Chocolate buttercream for filling and
    coating
Piping chocolate
    225g (8oz)
Melted chocolate
    60g (2oz)
Almond paste or sugarpaste
Vermicelli

Jelly diamonds
Small quantity of royal icing
Drinking straw
Round cake board 30.5cm (12")
Comb scraper
Piping tube No's. 1 and 13

HOW TO MAKE
PIPING CHOCOLATE

Ingredients:
Chocolate flavoured cake covering
    225g (8oz)

Glycerol
    ¼-½ teaspoon

Method
Place the chocolate in a heat-proof bowl
over a saucepan of simmering water and
stir until melted. Remove from heat
and stir in the glycerol, a little at a
time, until a soft piping consistency
is reached.

This delightful cake, decorated with
piped chocolate animals, will appeal
to all young children.

Colour the coconut with green food colouring and leave to dry for 1 hour.

Place sponge on cake board. Layer (see p.15) and coat with chocolate butter-cream. Decorate sides with comb scraper. Sprinkle coconut in centre and on base.

Make the piping chocolate (see above). Using the templates as guides, pipe the animal shapes onto waxed paper and leave to set.

Pipe the animals' features in royal icing (No. 1).

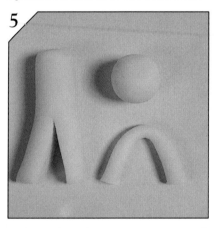

Roll out almond paste or sugarpaste and form the shapes for the figure, as shown. Leave to dry.

Decorate figure with melted chocolate, vermicelli and piped royal icing, as shown.

Fix the animals into the cake-top. Sprinkle green coconut around the base of each animal.

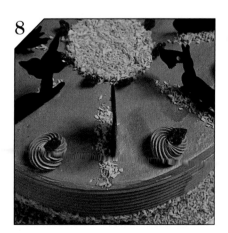

Pipe rosettes of chocolate buttercream around the cake-top (No. 13). Top each rosette with a jelly diamond.

Make a flag from paper and a drinking straw and pipe an inscription of choice. Fix, with the figure, to centre of cake-top, as shown.

TEMPLATES

ITEMS REQUIRED

Square fruit cake,
    20.5cm x 20.5cm (8" x 8")
    covered with almond paste
Royal icing
    455g (16oz)
Sugarpaste
    225g (8oz)
Assorted food colourings
Square cake board
    28cm x 28cm (11" x 11")
Comb scraper
Waxed paper
Fine paintbrush
Piping tube No's. 0, 1, 2, 3 and 43

NOTE: Royal icing without glycerine should be used for the runout figure.

This charming cake is ideal for any young lady, particularly as the items used to decorate the board can be varied to fit in with particular interests.

In Mary's design, all the items are created to appeal to a young girl but a teenager's cake could, for instance, have make-up, books, records and, perhaps, a much loved Teddy Bear instead.

The delightful runout figure on top of the cake is suitable for all ages.

Although Mary created this cake in pink for a girl, the colour scheme can be adapted to suit the favourite colour of the recipient and could, for example, have one colour icing on both the board and the cake, with the piped decoration in a different shade or another colour.

With a little imagination, many variations on the basic theme can be produced and the design, with an appropriate inscription, is suitable for celebration cakes of all kinds.

1

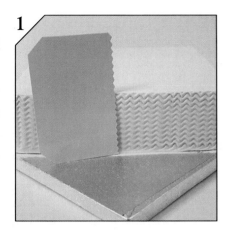

Place the almond paste covered cake (see p.13) diagonally on the cake board. Coat cake with royal icing, using a comb scraper for the sides on the final coat.

2

Spread royal icing over the cake board and stipple with a sponge. Leave to dry.

3

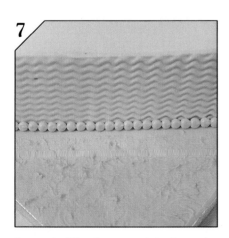

Place waxed paper over the template. Using an icing bag without a tube, pipe royal icing into the areas shown in the picture.

4

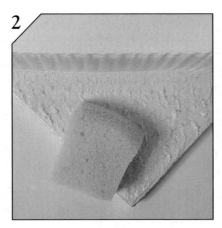

Continue piping royal icing into the further parts, as shown.

5

Finish piping in the remaining parts with royal icing and leave to dry for 12 hours.

6

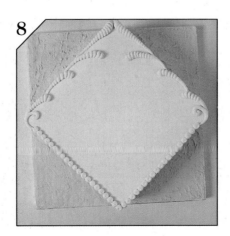

Pipe detail onto the figure in royal icing (No. 0). Paint the features with edible food colouring using a fine paintbrush.

7

Pipe a shell border around the base of the cake (No. 3).

8

Pipe a series of scrolls and shells in royal icing around the cake-top edge (No's. 43 and 3).

9

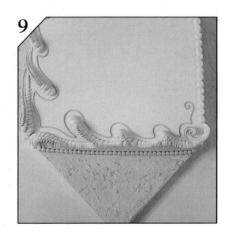

Pipe lines beside the scrolls, then overpipe the scrolls, as shown (No's. 3 and 2).

10

Carefully remove the figure from the waxed paper and fix to the cake-top, using a little royal icing. Pipe the ground and flowers in royal icing (No. 1).

11

Pipe and decorate inscription of choice (No. 1).

12

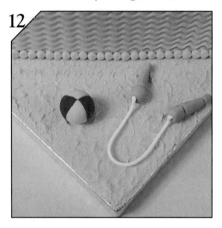

Make a ball and skipping rope from sugarpaste. Fix the pieces to one corner of the cake board with royal icing.

13

Make 2 figures from sugarpaste. Fix the figures to another corner of the cake board with royal icing.

14

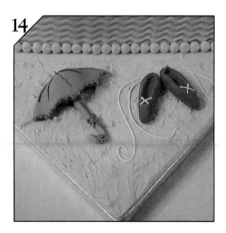

Make a parasol and ballet shoes from sugarpaste and fix to the third corner with royal icing. Pipe the shoe laces in royal icing (No. 1).

15

Make one large and one small teddy bear from sugarpaste and fix to the remaining corner of the cake board with royal icing.

ZONKER

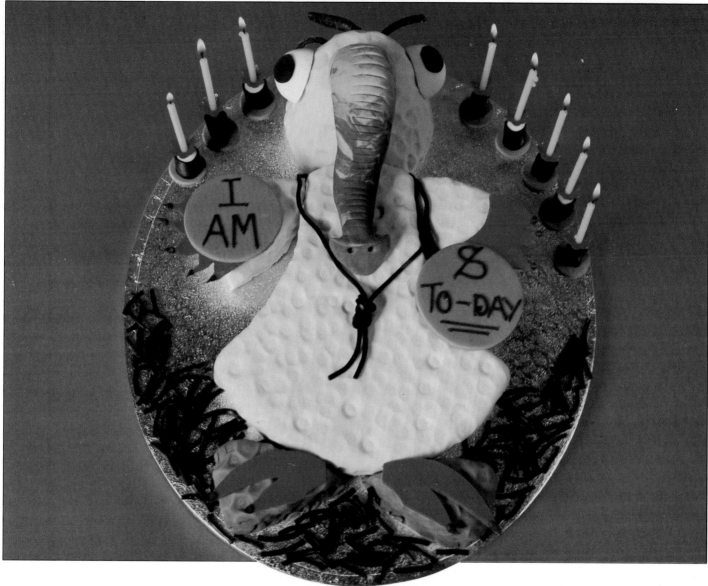

ITEMS REQUIRED

Round sponge
    20.5 cm (8")

Sponge made in a 225g (½ pint)
    pudding basin

Jam and buttercream for filling and
    coating

Sugarpaste
    680g (1½lb)

Assorted food colourings

Small quantity of royal icing

Liquorice strips

Oval cake board
    35.5cm x 30.5cm (14" x 12")

Small rolling pin

Piping tube No. 1

Monsters have always delighted
children of all ages and Mary
created this cute fellow to appeal to
teenagers as well as to younger
children.

Although the finished cake looks
complex, it is very easy to make
as the textured 'skin' is quickly
achieved by impressing sugarpaste
with the end of a small rolling pin or
a wooden spoon.

The impressive trunk, also made
from sugarpaste, is easily moulded
and marked with a knife.

Liquorice strips add the finishing
touches, and have the advantage of
being a favourite with children.

1

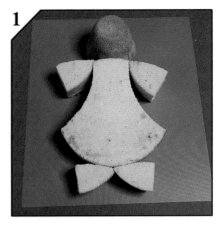

Cut the sponge to the shapes shown. Cut and layer the sponges (see step 2 on p.15) and coat all pieces with buttercream.

2

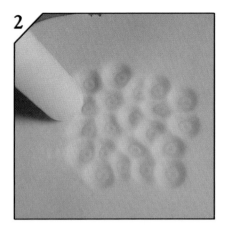

Roll out sufficient sugarpaste to cover the head, arms and body pieces. Indent the paste with a small rolling pin to form a pattern.

3

Cover the pieces with the patterned sugarpaste, and cover the feet, as shown. Arrange the covered sponge pieces on the cake board.

4

Half-mix colour into some sugarpaste and make a trunk. Moisten and fix to the face.

5

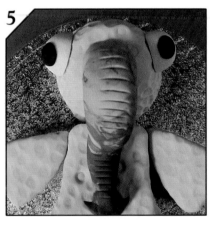

Make a pair of protruding eyes from sugarpaste. Moisten and fix to the side of the head.

6

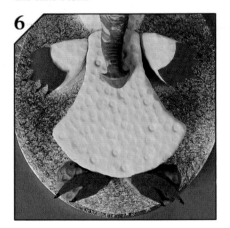

Make the hands and feet from sugarpaste. Moisten and fix, as shown.

7

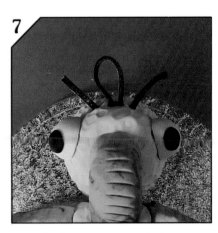

To make the antennae, push the liquorice sticks into the paste on top of the head.

8

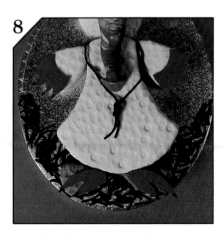

Complete the decoration of the monster and board with more liquorice sticks.

9

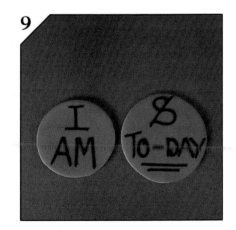

Cut two sugarpaste plaques. Pipe inscription of choice onto plaques (No. 1). Moisten and fix to monster's hands. Fix candles and holders to the board.

KITE

ITEMS REQUIRED

Round sponge
    25.5cm (10")
Jam and buttercream for filling and
    coating
Grated chocolate
    115g (4oz)
Sugarpaste
    170g (6oz)
Assorted food colourings
Royal icing
    455g (16oz)
Round cake board
    35.5cm (14")
Piping tube No's. 1, 2, 3 and 43
Length of narrow ribbon

NOTE: Royal icing without glycerine
should be used for runout work.

Kite flying is an extremely popular
sport with all ages and this cake
could be coloured to match the
recipient's own kite.

1

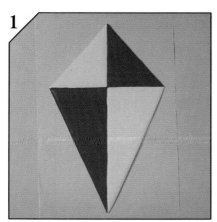

Outline, and fill in, a kite on waxed
paper using 2 colours of royal icing.
Leave to dry for 24 hours.

2

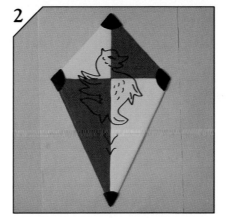

Using the template as a guide, pipe
design onto kite in royal icing, or
design of choice (No. 1). Make corner
pieces from sugarpaste and fix, as shown.

3

Cut and layer the sponge (see step 2 on
p.15) and coat with buttercream. Cover
the sides with grated chocolate and place
towards the back of the cake board.

4

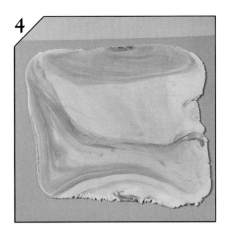

Half-mix food colouring into the sugarpaste and roll out to form sky effect.

5

Cut and position the sugarpaste to fit the cake-top. Cover the cake board with a thin layer of royal icing and stipple with a fine sponge.

6

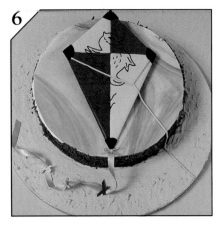

Fix the kite to the cake-top using royal icing. Pipe the kite strings (No. 3) and fix a ribbon to the end.

7

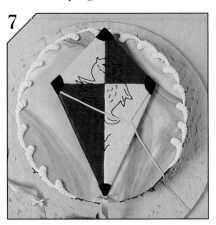

Pipe a series of 'C' scrolls in royal icing around the cake-top edge as shown (No. 43).

8

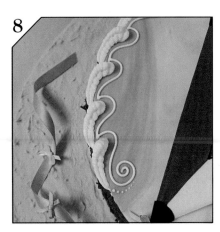

Pipe a line beside the scrolls, then overpipe each scroll with royal icing (No. 2).

9

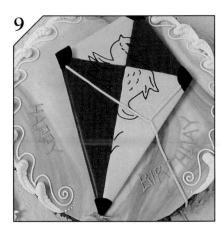

Pipe inscription of choice onto cake-top using royal icing (No. 1).

ZOO-TIME

ITEMS REQUIRED

Hexagonal sponge cake
    20.5cm (8")
    coated with a thin layer of
    almond paste and royal icing

Royal icing (with glycerine) for piping
    225g (8oz)

Royal icing (without glycerine) for
    runouts 340g (12oz)

Assorted food colourings

Piping tube No's. 1, 2 and 43

Round cake board
    30.5cm (12")

NOTE: Royal icing without glycerine
should be used for runout and No. 1
work.

This unusual hexagonal cake
demonstrates the technique of royal
icing a cake and then attaching
runout figures to it.

The runouts are easy to make,
although they take a little time to
prepare and require time to dry.
They can, however, be made in
advance and stored in a cardboard
box in a dry place. They will keep
for several months when stored in
this way.

The colour scheme for this cake is
very much a matter of choice and

can be adapted to the child's
favourite colour.

This cake would be suitable for
children aged from 3 to 10.

1

RUNOUTS: Using the template as a guide, pipe the outline for the monkey in royal icing onto waxed paper (No. 1).

2

Using a piping bag without a tube, fill in the outline with royal icing and leave to dry for 24 hours. Then, pipe or paint in the details.

3

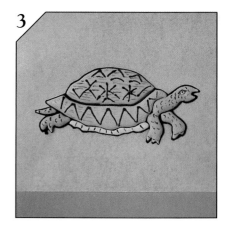

Repeat steps 1-2 to complete the tortoise.

4

Following steps 1-2, complete the lion and decorate as shown.

5

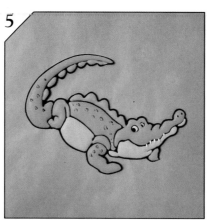

Colour the royal icing in shades of green and follow steps 1-2 when piping the alligator. Decorate as shown.

6

Following steps 1-2, complete the hippopotamus and decorate as shown.

7

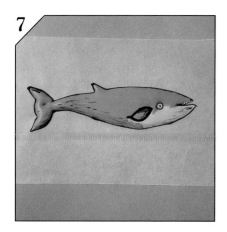

Following steps 1-2, complete the whale and decorate as shown.

8

Following steps 1-2, complete the horse and decorate as shown.

9

Remove the animals from the waxed paper. Fix the monkey to the caketop with royal icing. Pipe branches (No. 1) and leaves in royal icing using a leaf bag.

10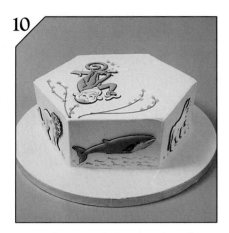

Fix 3 other animal shapes to the cake-sides, using royal icing. Pipe appropriate scenery under each figure (No. 1).

11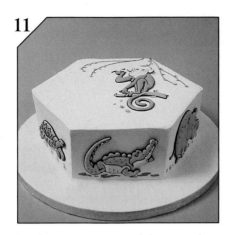

Fix the remaining animal shapes to the other cake-sides. Decorate with scenery (No. 1).

12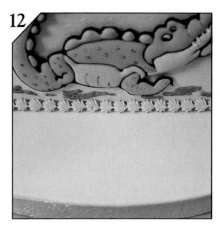

Pipe a shell border along the base of the cake (No. 43), as shown.

13

Pipe decoration and inscription of choice in royal icing onto cake-top (No.1).

14

Pipe a series of scrolls and shells in royal icing around the edge of the cake-top (No. 43).

15

Pipe a line beside the scrolls, then overpipe each scroll in royal icing, as shown (No. 2).

16

Pipe the name of each animal in royal icing onto the cake board (No. 1).

17

Pipe branches in royal icing under each animal name (No. 1).

18

Complete the decoration by piping leaves on the branches in royal icing, using a leaf bag.

TEMPLATES

SKATEBOARD

ITEMS REQUIRED

Sponge made in a
905g (2lb) loaf tin

Jam and buttercream for filling and
coating

Sugarpaste
340g (12oz)

Assorted food colourings

Compound or cooking chocolate
340g (12oz)

Small quantity of royal icing

Almond paste for figure
115g (4oz)

Rectangular cake board
30.5cm x 25.5cm (12" x 10")

Piping tube No's. 1, 2 and 3
Birthday candles and holders

This cake is the ideal choice for a
teenage skateboard enthusiast
although it can, of course, be made
for the younger skateboarder as well.

The design uses the simple technique of melted chocolate to form
the board, which is placed on the
cake itself.

To personalise the cake, the
sugarpaste figure could be coloured
to represent a favourite outfit of the
birthday boy, and careful piping of
the features could even suggest a
'look-alike' face.

1

Bake the sponge in the 905g (2lb) sponge tin and leave to cool on a wire tray. Cut and layer the sponge (see step 2 on p.15).

2

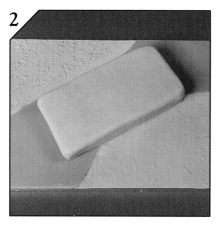

Cut road from sugarpaste, moisten and fix to cake board. Cover remaining area with royal icing and stipple. Cover the sponge with sugarpaste (see p.12).

3

Make the wheels from sugarpaste. Moisten and fix to the cake as shown.

4

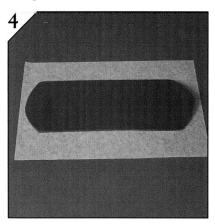

Melt chocolate over a pan of warm water. Spread melted chocolate onto grease-proof paper and leave to set. Cut out skateboard shape from the set chocolate.

5

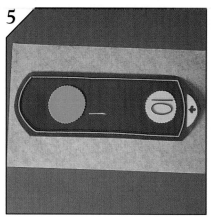

Cut 2 circles from sugarpaste and fix to the chocolate. Decorate the skateboard by piping lines and inscription of choice in royal icing (No. 2).

6

Fix the chocolate to the cake-top, using royal icing.

7

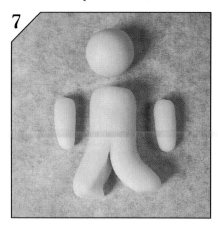

To make the figure, form a roll of almond paste for the body and cut one end to form legs. Make a ball of paste for the head, and 2 rolls for the arms. Leave to dry.

8

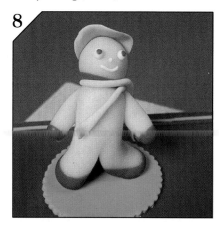

Dip hands and feet into melted chocolate. Make a hat and scarf from sugarpaste and pipe features in royal icing (No. 1). Fix figure to sugarpaste circle.

9

Pipe inscription of choice onto chocolate skateboard (No. 1). Complete by fixing birthday candles and holders on the board, as shown.

EASTER BONNET

ITEMS REQUIRED

Sponge mixture
    400g (14oz)

Oven-proof pudding basin
    1 litre (2 pints)

Jam and buttercream for filling and
    coating

Sugarpaste
    455g (16oz)

Assorted food colourings

Round cake board
    30.5cm (12")

Small crimper

Spray of sugar flowers

Feathers

Narrow ribbon

This delicate cake is ideal for young
ladies of any age and it would make
an ideal teenager's birthday cake as
well as appealing to young
children.

The bonnet, which is extremely easy
to make, is decorated with sugar
flowers, which should be made in
advance and allowed to dry
thoroughly.

The Mary Ford book "Decorative
Sugar Flowers for Cakes" gives
instructions for making many
different types of sugar flowers.

Alternatively, a spray of silk flowers
could be used to complete the
decoration.

1 Bake the sponge in the oven-proof pudding basin. Turn out and leave to cool.

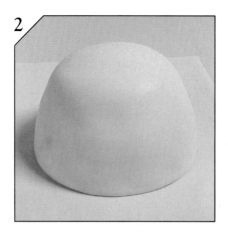

2 Trim the sponge, cut and layer (see step 2 on p.15). Coat the sponge with buttercream. Cover the sponge with sugarpaste, as shown (see p.12).

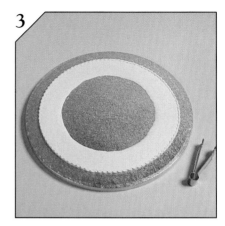

3 Cut the hat brim from sugarpaste. Fix to cake board and decorate the outer edge, using the crimper.

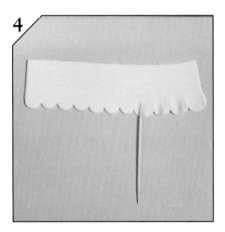

4 Cut a strip of sugarpaste with a scalloped edge. Frill the scalloped edge by rolling a cocktail stick backwards and forwards along the edge.

5 Moisten the frill with water and fix it to the inner edge of the brim.

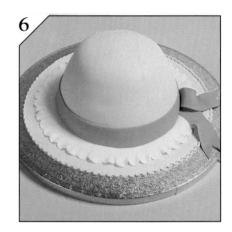

6 Place the cake in the centre of the frill to form the crown. Make a ribbon of sugarpaste. Moisten and fix to the crown, as shown.

7 Cut flower shapes from sugarpaste. Moisten the flowers and fix to the crown of the bonnet, as shown.

8 Fix a spray of sugar flowers, with ribbon, onto the brim at the front of the bonnet.

9 Fix more sugar flowers, ribbon and feathers to the knot in the ribbon to complete the bonnet.

FOOTBALL

ITEMS REQUIRED

Sponge
   455g (16oz)
Round pudding basin
   1 litre (2 pint)
Jam and buttercream for filling and
   coating
Sugarpaste
   570g (1¼lb)
Assorted food colourings
Small quantity of royal icing
Square cake board
   30.5cm x 30.5cm (12" x 12")

Piping tube No. 1
Narrow ribbon
Plastic football players

This is the cake for a football-mad youngster as the model footballers can be selected to match the favourite team colours.

The cake is surprisingly easy to make and the ball and board are quickly but effectively decorated using, sugarpaste.

The secret of success lies in using a round pudding basin. Mary used the two halves of a metal Christmas pudding mould.

This adaptable cake can be made for any age.

1

Divide the sponge mixture equally between the two halves of the round pudding basin, and bake. Allow to cool.

2

Trim and cut the sponges. Spread with jam and buttercream and place one on top of the other. Coat with buttercream. Place in refrigerator for 2 hours.

3

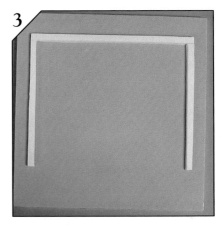

Cover the cake board with a thin layer of sugarpaste. Cut 3 narrow strips of sugarpaste, moisten and fix to the board to form a goal post.

4

Carefully cover the sponge with sugarpaste, as shown, to form the football.

5

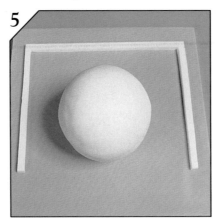

Place the ball in the centre of the cake board, between the goal post.

6

Cut sugarpaste shapes, as shown. Moisten and fix around the ball to form an even pattern.

7

Make 2 linesmen's flags from different coloured sugarpaste and fix to the board, as shown.

8

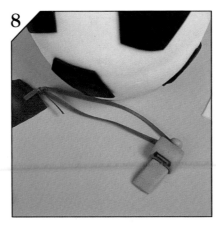

Make a whistle from sugarpaste and fix to the board. Attach a loop of narrow ribbon to the whistle.

9

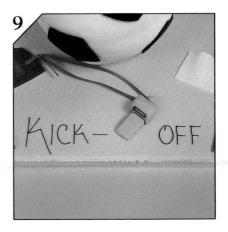

Pipe inscription of choice onto the cake board (No. 1). Complete by fixing the footballers along one edge, using royal icing.

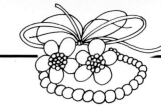

ITEMS REQUIRED

Round fruit cake,
    18cm (7")
    covered with almond paste and
    coated in royal icing
Sugarpaste
    115g (4oz)
Assorted food colourings
Royal icing
    455g (16oz)
Cake board
    7.5cm (3") larger than cake
Piping tube No's. 0, 1, and 2
Ribbons of choice

NOTE: Royal icing without glycerine should be used for runouts and No. 1 work.

This delicate royal iced cake, which is easy to make, would please any dainty young girl.

The colour scheme can be chosen to match a party dress or a favourite shade, with the flowers being coloured appropriately.

Although this design has been prepared on a fruit cake, a royal iced sponge could also be used if preferred.

This beautiful cake would delight the heart of darling daughters aged between 8 and 18.

1 Cut 60 sugarpaste blossoms and shape with the end of a paintbrush or wooden spoon. Leave to set. Pipe centres with royal icing (No. 1).

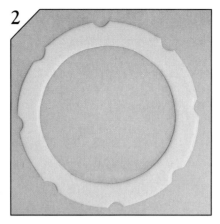

2 Using the template as a guide, pipe the outline onto waxed paper (No. 1) and fill in with soft royal icing to make the top runout. Leave to dry for 24 hours.

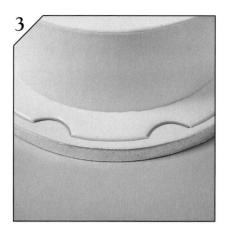

3 To make the base runout, pipe the outline onto board (No. 2) and fill in between outline and cake-base with royal icing. Leave to dry for 24 hours.

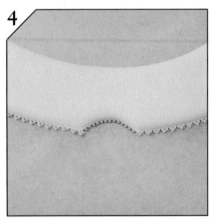

4 Pipe a series of dots around the outer edge of the top runout (No. 0). Leave to dry for 12 hours.

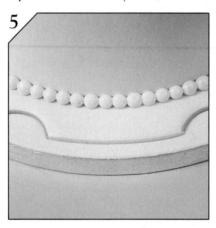

5 Pipe bulbs of royal icing around the base of the cake (No. 2).

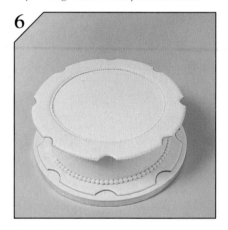

6 Remove the top runout from the waxed paper and fix to the cake-top with royal icing. Pipe dots of royal icing along the inside edge (No. 1).

7 Fix the blossoms and ribbons to the cake-top, using royal icing.

8 Pipe and decorate inscription of choice (No. 1) in royal icing.

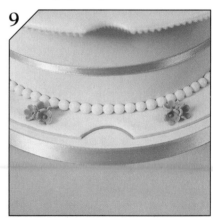

9 Fix blossoms to the base runout. Fix a ribbon around the cake-side, and around the edge of the cake board.

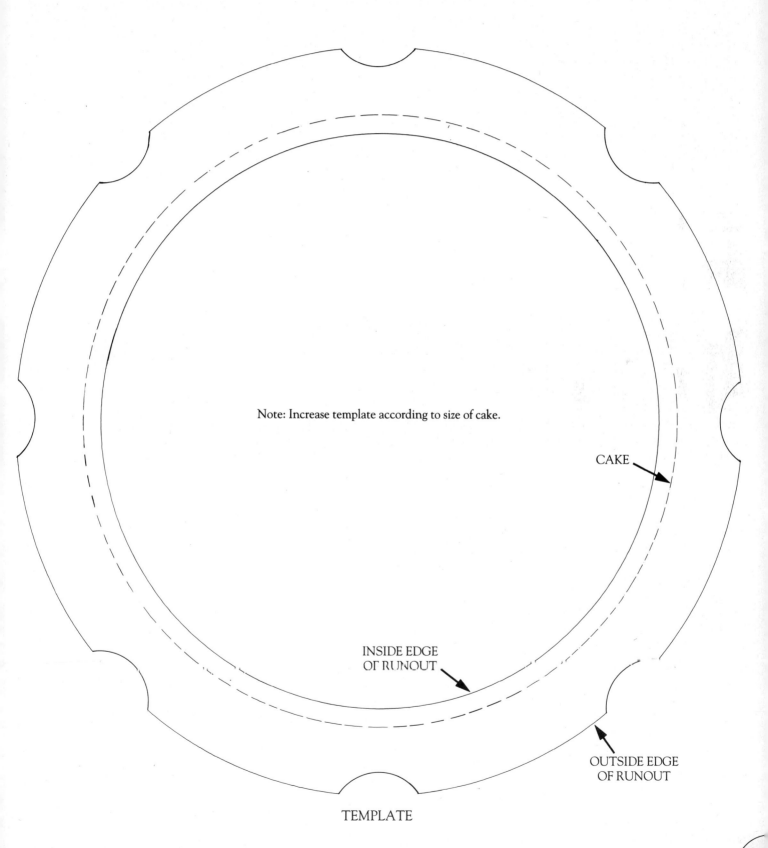

Note: Increase template according to size of cake.

CAKE

INSIDE EDGE
OF RUNOUT

OUTSIDE EDGE
OF RUNOUT

TEMPLATE

PARTY CAKE

ITEMS REQUIRED

Square sponge
    20.5cm x 20.5cm (8" x 8")

Jam for filling

Orange and lemon buttercream for
    filling, coating and decorating

Toasted flaked almonds

Chocolate buttons
    (half in white chocolate)

Small quantity of royal icing

Food colourings

Orange and lemon jelly segments

Square cake board
    25.5cm x 25.5cm (10" x 10")

Piping tube No's. 1, 13 and 7

Birthday candles and holders

This is an attractive party cake
which is extremely quick and simple
to make, especially as the chocolate
buttons and orange and lemon slices
used are all easily purchased.

The simple design will be much
appreciated by busy mums who want
to achieve a professional finish
without much difficulty.

This party cake is a versatile design
which would appeal to all young
children and would be particularly
appropriate to accompany a birthday
visit to a show.

1 Cut and layer the sponge (see step 2 on p.15). Coat the top and sides with orange buttercream. Coat the sides with toasted flaked almonds and place cake on board.

2 Pipe faces onto the chocolate buttons in royal icing (No. 1). Use brown royal icing to pipe the white chocolate buttons.

3 Make a number of clown heads by cutting the jelly segments and fixing them to the cake-top with the chocolate buttons. Pipe detail in royal icing (No. 1).

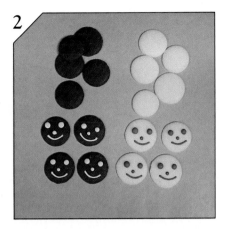

4 Pipe a large rosette of lemon buttercream (No. 13) in the centre of the cake and fix chocolate buttons, as shown.

5 Complete the central decoration by fixing jelly segments to the buttercream rosette. Place more buttons on top and pipe, as shown (No. 1).

6 Pipe small rosettes of buttercream around the edge of the cake-top. Place half a chocolate button onto each pair of rosettes.

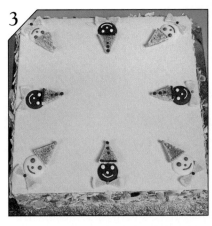

7 Pipe inscription of choice onto the chocolate buttons (No. 1) and leave to dry.

8 Pipe rosettes of buttercream around the edge of the cake board (No. 7).

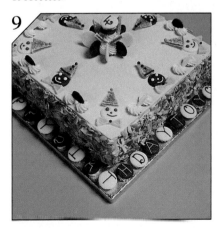

9 Top each rosette with a piped chocolate button to spell out inscription of choice. Complete the party cake by adding the relevant number of candles and holders.

TWINKLE TOES

ITEMS REQUIRED

Oval fruit cake
    20.5cm (8")
    covered with almond paste and
    coated in royal icing

Assorted food colourings
Piping tube No's. 1, 2 and 42
Cake board
    30.5cm x 23cm (12" x 9")

NOTE: Royal icing without glycerine
should be used for the butterflies.

This dainty cake has been specially
created to delight all young girls, but
would particularly appeal to those
who enjoy dancing or fairy tales.

The oval royal iced cake is decorated with easy-to-make piped
butterflies and the outlined figure of
the fairy.

The cake could, however, be
adapted by using any suitable

template figure in the centre and
piping an appropriate inscription
around it.

The design could also be used on a
royal iced sponge cake if preferred.

1

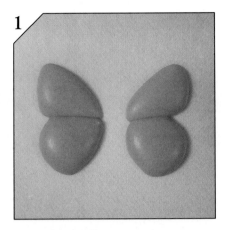

Using the template as a guide, pipe several butterfly wings in royal icing onto waxed paper and leave to dry for 24 hours.

2

Pipe the butterfly bodies onto waxed paper and, before they dry, fix the decorated wings (No. 2). Leave to dry for 24 hours.

3

Position the cake on the cake board. Pipe an outline onto board and fill in with royal icing to make a decorative border (No. 2).

4

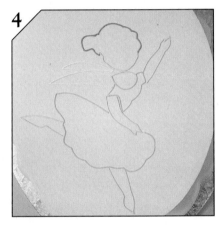

Using the Twinkle Toes template, or template of choice, outline the motif in royal icing on the cake-top (No. 1).

5

Complete the motif with further detail, as shown (No. 1).

6

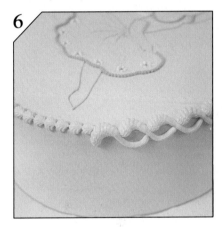

Pipe a series of 'S' scrolls and shells in royal icing around the top edge of the cake (No. 42).

7

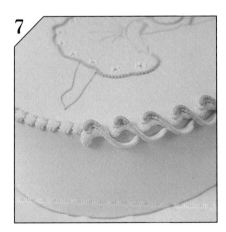

Overpipe the 'S' scrolls using royal icing (No. 2), then overpipe each scroll (No. 1).

8

Fix the butterflies to the cake-top using royal icing. Pipe inscription of choice (No. 1).

9

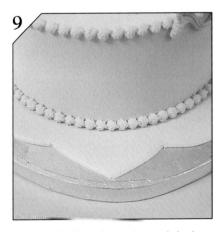

Pipe shells of royal icing around the base of the cake and decorate as shown (No. 42 and No. 1).

TEMPLATES

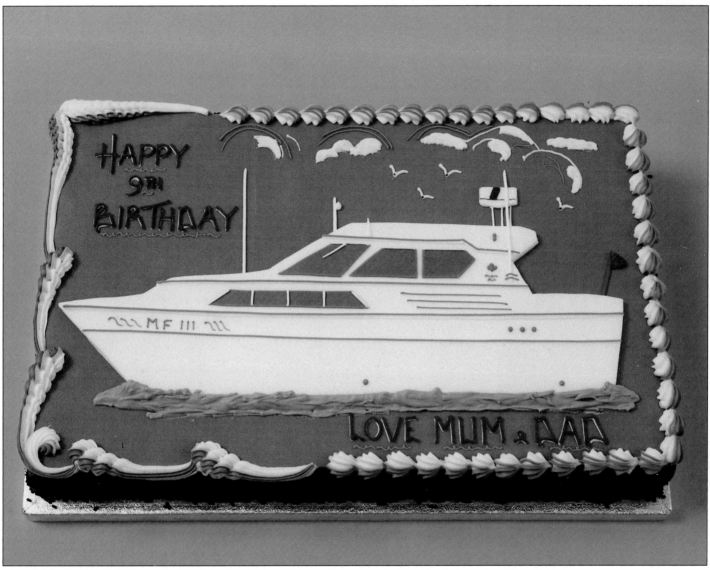

ITEMS REQUIRED

2 sponges made in a swiss roll tin
    28cm x 18cm (11" x 7")

Chocolate buttercream
    170g (6oz)

Vermicelli
    115g (4oz)

Sugarpaste
    225g (8oz)

Royal icing
    115g (4oz)

Assorted food colourings

Cake board
    30.5cm x 20.5cm (12" x 8")

Piping tube No's. 1, 2 and 7

Mary has designed this cake with a nautical theme that will appeal to all age groups, from children as young as 5, to any adult who enjoys taking to the water.

As well as the motor boat shown, any type of boat can be cut out from sugarpaste, from a small fishing or rowing boat, to a sleek ocean-going racer in full sail for the youngster who likes to dream.

A fruit cake, covered with almond paste and sugarpaste, could be used as the basis for this cake but the vermicelli should be omitted from the sides.

1

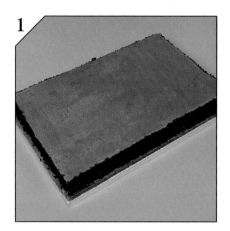

Layer the 2 sponges (see step 2 on p.15) and coat top and sides with chocolate buttercream. Cover the cake-top with sugarpaste, and the sides with vermicelli.

2

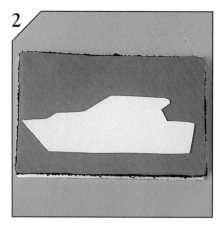

Using the template as a guide, cut out sugarpaste boat. Moisten and fix to the cake-top.

3

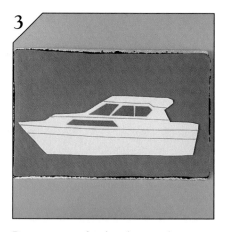

Begin to pipe the detail in royal icing (No. 1). Cut out windows from sugarpaste. Moisten and fix to the boat, as shown.

4

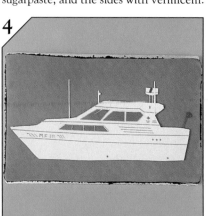

Make a radar reflector from sugarpaste. Moisten and fix, as shown. Pipe further details in royal icing (No. 1).

5

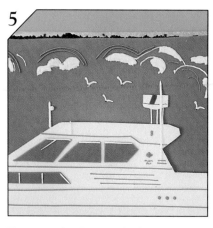

To create the sky, pipe birds and clouds in royal icing (No. 1).

6

Pipe, and then overpipe, inscription of choice in the top left hand corner of the cake (No. 1).

7

Pipe the water in royal icing. Pipe, and then overpipe, inscription of choice in the bottom right hand corner of the cake.

8

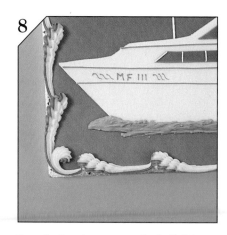

Pipe the boat's name on the hull (No. 1). Using royal icing in 2 colours, pipe a series of scrolls part way around the the cake-top edge (No. 7).

9

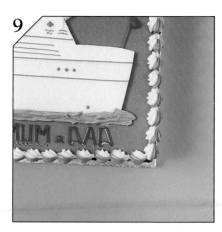

Complete the decoration by piping shells of royal icing around the remaining edge of the cake-top (No. 7).

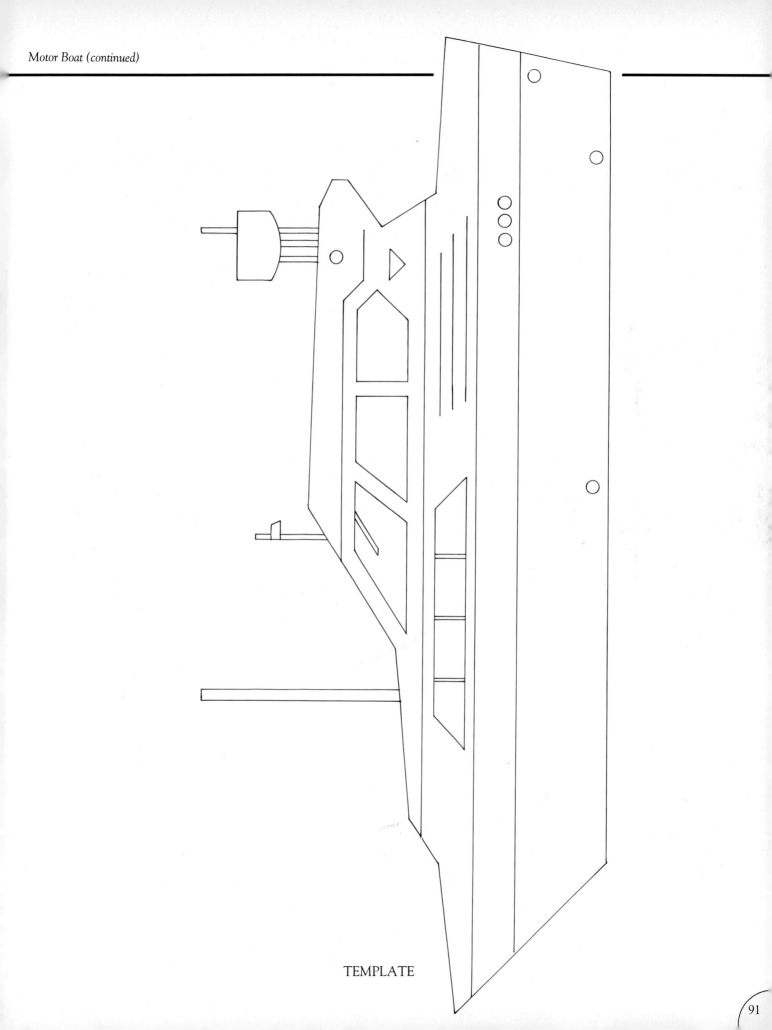

TEMPLATE

FROSTY SNOWMEN

ITEMS REQUIRED

Round fruit cake
    20.5cm (8") coated in almond
    paste and royal icing with
    combed sides

Meringues for snowmen

Royal icing
    455g (16oz)

Assorted food colourings

Sugarpaste
    115g (4oz)

Savoy piping bag and
    1cm (½") tube

Piping tube No's. 1, 2 and 4

Round cake board
    38cm (15")

MERINGUE SNOWMEN

Ingredients:
Egg whites
    (Size 3)   2
Caster sugar
    115g (4oz)

Method:
As for Toadstools (see steps 1-3 on
p. 53).

Bake at 100°C (200°F), or gas mark ¼,
for approximately 2-2½ hours or until
the outside is firm and crisp.

This charming royal iced cake,
decorated with easily-made
meringue snowmen, is ideal for a
Christmas birthday. The snowmen
could be given to the guests to take
home afterwards.

If kept in an airtight tin, the
snowmen can be made well in
advance of the big day to save time.
The cake can then be assembled a
day or two before the party.

This design can also be used on a
sponge cake if preferred.

1

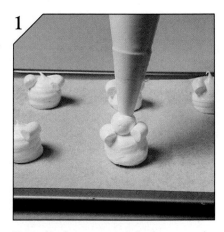

To make the snowmen's bodies, pipe the meringue mixture onto a baking tray lined with silicone paper.

2

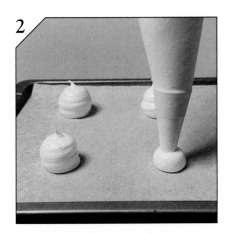

Pipe the snowmen's arms and heads and bake as instructed.

3

When cold, decorate the snowmen with royal icing and pieces of sugarpaste, as shown.

4

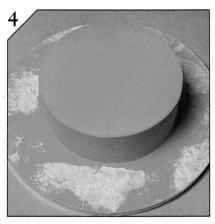

Coat the board in royal icing. When the icing is dry, stipple with a sponge to form snow.

5

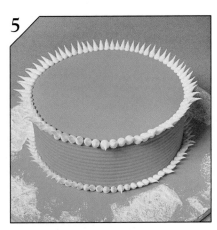

Pipe spikes of royal icing around the edge of the cake-top and base, to simulate icicles (No. 4).

6

Cut a round plaque from sugarpaste. Fix a snowman to the plaque, using royal icing. Pipe small spiked icicles around plaque edge (No. 2).

7

Pipe inscription of choice around cake-top, as shown (No. 1).

8

Fix the remaining snowmen around the edge of the cake board, using royal icing.

9

Pipe bulbs of stiff royal icing between the snowmen on the cake board (No. 4) and fix a candle into each bulb.

CRACKER

ITEMS REQUIRED

Vanilla Swiss roll

Chocolate Swiss roll

Royal icing
    225g (8oz)

Assorted food colourings

Jam and buttercream for filling and
    coating

Sugarpaste
    455g (16oz)

Piping tube No's. 1 and 42

Round cake board
    30.5cm (12")

Doyley
    30.5cm (12")

This attractive Christmas Cracker
sponge is surrounded by individual
fairy cakes on which have been
piped the party guests' names. They
make a delightful present to take
home after the party.

1 Using a piping bag without a tube and
using the template as a guide, pipe the
Father Christmas in royal icing (without
glycerine) onto waxed paper, as shown.

2 Finish piping the Father Christmas, as
shown, and leave to dry for 24 hours.
When dry, paint in the features with
food colouring.

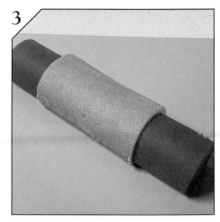

3 Fill the Swiss rolls with jam and buttercream and roll up. Cut the chocolate swiss
roll in half and fix to each end of the
vanilla Swiss roll. Coat with buttercream.

4

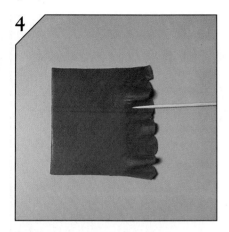

Cut 2 pieces of sugarpaste for the cracker ends. Frill one edge of each piece, using a cocktail stick.

6

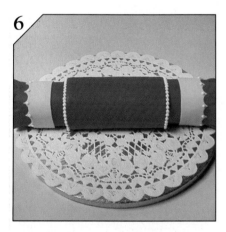

Cut 2 decorative sugarpaste bands. Moisten and fix the bands to the frilled ends. Decorate with piped royal icing, as shown (No's. 1 and 42).

8

Make holly leaves from sugarpaste. Moisten and fix to the decorative bands at each end. Pipe the berries (No. 1).

5

Cover the vanilla Swiss roll with sugarpaste. Fix the frilled sugarpaste pieces to the chocolate Swiss rolls and place on the cake board with the doyley.

7

Cut a plaque from sugarpaste and frill the edge. Moisten and fix to the cracker. Pipe on inscription of choice and fix bows of ribbon and Father Christmas runout.

9

Decorate the fairy cakes with piped names, sugarpaste holly leaves and bows of ribbon.

INDEX